Coaching with Powerful Interactions

So much more than a book! See page 9 for information about accessing coaching videos and other bonus material.

Coaching with Powerful Interactions

A Guide to Partnering with Early Childhood Teachers

Judy Jablon, Amy Laura Dombro, and Shaun Johnsen

National Association for the Education of Young Children
Washington, DC

naeyc®

National Association for the
Education of Young Children
1313 L Street NW, Suite 500
Washington, DC 20005-4101
202-232-8777 • 800-424-2460
www.naeyc.org

NAEYC Books

Editor-in-Chief
Kathy Charner

Senior Creative Design Manager
Audra Meckstroth

Managing Editor
Mary Jaffe

Senior Editor
Holly Bohart

Creative Design Specialist
Malini Dominey

Editorial Assistant
Ryan Smith

Through its publications
program, the National
Association for the Education
of Young Children (NAEYC)
provides a forum for discussion
of major issues and ideas in the
early childhood field, with the
hope of provoking thought and
promoting professional growth.
The views expressed or implied
in this book are not necessarily
those of the Association or its
members.

**Coaching with Powerful Interactions: A Guide to Partnering with
Early Childhood Teachers**

Library of Congress Control Number: 2015955514

ISBN: 978-1-938113-19-2

Item 2451

Contents

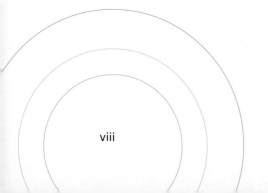

Preface

In 2011, NAEYC published *Powerful Interactions: How to Connect with Children to Extend Their Learning*. As we teach about Powerful Interactions, we continue to learn from everyone because interactions are an important part of life. Even before this book was published, many of our colleagues acknowledged that using Powerful Interactions with adults would be helpful in their work.

Friends and family pointed out that "static" interferes with quality interactions at home, not just in the workplace. In many conversations, we began to explore how "extend learning" isn't just something we do as we teach children. It can be part of the richness of collegial partnerships and friendships when trust exists. Learning more about Powerful Interactions between and among adults and how learning partnerships can lead to growth and learning inspired us to write this guide for you.

In collaboration with early childhood colleagues from New Jersey to Arkansas to Arizona and Hawaii, we have created this book to share what we are learning about Powerful Interactions between and among adults. We hope you will see yourself reflected in these pages and video clips and recognized as having the strengths you demonstrate each day in your work as a coach. Our goal is to share coaching principles, strategies, and stories that will inspire and motivate you to build on your strengths and make your practice even more effective.

Like you, we have each worked with teachers of young children. Our work as early childhood coaches, writers, and consultants (Judy and Amy) and as a video producer (Shaun) has taken us together and separately to a wide variety of settings. Whether in an

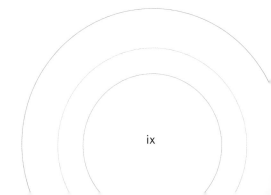

Early Head Start program, infant and toddler caregiving setting, preschool, or kindergarten program, the goal of our work is to have meaningful interactions with teachers that build on their strengths and promote positive changes in their practice, which will impact children's well-being and learning.

Like you, we have had our own successes and struggles in having meaningful interactions with teachers. As you use this guide, we invite you to share with us the effective interactions you have had as a coach and how you are becoming even more effective in your practice by transforming everyday interactions with teachers into Powerful Interactions.

Here are some of our stories that have shaped our thinking:

Judy: Thinking back to my first visit to Ms. Jones's room 25 years ago, what I remember most clearly is me—how I felt and how I acted.

My nervousness. How would I help her? Would I know what to say? She was older than me. Would she take me seriously?

My impressions. I thought her room was cluttered, that the furniture needed to be rearranged to create clearly defined learning centers.

My disappointment. She was not pleased to see me. She did not even stop what she was doing to chat with me after I had driven for two hours in heavy traffic to get to her school, worried the whole time that I would be late. (During that time, she was preparing for the day and greeting 20 preschoolers as they took off their coats and boots on a hectic winter morning.)

As a "staff developer"—that's what we were called 25 years ago—I believed my job was to offer teachers tips and strategies based on my observations of their gaps. I'm not sure where that belief came from. What I do know is that very few teachers were receptive. Some were tolerant, and others were hostile—either ignoring me outright or not showing up on the days I was assigned to visit their classrooms.

As a teacher of young children, I hadn't thought that my job was to "dispense knowledge" or to look for "gaps" and fill them. As a graduate student at Bank Street College of Education and then later as a teacher in the Bank Street School for Children, I learned from my mentors to listen for children's strengths and interests, then respond by creating

Coaching with Powerful Interactions

opportunities that would spark their curiosity, invite thinking, and encourage questions. I loved teaching this way with children, yet when I began supporting adult learners, I didn't apply these same ideas. When I talk with many others who support adult learning, they describe similar insights.

From that first visit to Ms. Jones's classroom to the present, I have learned over and over again that with both children and adults, our work as educators is to facilitate learning. No matter how young or old we are, learning happens because we want to make it happen. We have a desire, a curiosity, an interest in refining a skill or learning a new one.

Adult learners want to be validated for what they already know, recognized for their strengths and experience. When they feel that families, colleagues, supervisors, and coaches see and appreciate them, they are more likely to risk a bit of vulnerability to ask questions and stretch their thinking and practice. I deeply appreciate what Ms. Jones and so many other teachers have helped me to learn: My job as an educator is to help to make that happen.

I neglected to help Ms. Jones to see her strengths because my focus was on me. I was inexperienced and worried, asking myself, "How am I doing?" It's taken time and practice to learn how to quiet "me" and focus on the teacher, notice her moments of effectiveness, and invite her to talk about her decision making. That's the basis for the conversation between us. I now appreciate that in coaching conversations like this we both learn, and I am deeply grateful that I continue to learn every day from the conversations I have with all the colleagues I meet.

Recently a workshop participant helped me to become more "consciously competent" about an essential lesson of this journey. It was the second day of a workshop about Powerful Interactions coaching. The participant, Robin, offered an insight she had taken from the first day: "Judy, you made a comment yesterday that stuck with me and that I know is my biggest take-away. You said: 'I've learned that I just have to get over myself.'"

I didn't realize I had said that the day before, nor did I expect it to be the "major insight" someone would take away. But, because Robin called my attention to it, I came to see that it is a huge take-away for me from the last 25 years. I can be most effective in my work when I am willing to get over myself!

It's taken time and practice to learn how to quiet "me" and focus on the teacher.

Amy: The seeds for my work around Powerful Interactions were planted when I headed the Infant and Family Center at Bank Street College of Education. I can still picture clearly the day two consultants came to visit, dressed in well-pressed blouses, skirts, stockings, and low heels (it was back in the '70s).

I greeted them with a baby on my shoulder and smears of playdough and baby food on my shirt. I pulled over two chairs and invited them to sit and observe for a while. It was a busy day. Of course things always felt busier when there were visitors, but this day the baby on my shoulder was teething and fussy and Jonah, a toddler, needed lots of help to remember not to bite, which had my coteacher and me on alert.

That morning we had decided to divide the group. My coteacher would take Jonah and another child to the corner market to buy some fruit for snack, and I'd "stay home" with the teething baby and three other children who would all have a turn to go outside later in the day. That way, Jonah would get a break from the group and a little extra attention, I'd be able to offer the baby a teething ring from the freezer, and we'd all get a little break from whole group life.

I noticed the visitors taking notes, then turned my attention back to the children. I helped the shoppers get on their way with only one "biting hurts" reminder to Jonah and then picked a few books off the shelf to read to the children who were interested in a story.

As we settled down to read (with two toddlers and the teething baby on my lap), our visitors stood up to go. I smiled and said goodbye. One of them gestured that she wanted to talk with me. I gave the book to the toddlers who were reading with me and said I'd be right back. With the infant still in my arms and an additional smear on my shirt, I went over to talk with her.

"Thank you," she said. "We enjoyed our visit. But I think the water table would be better used if you moved it over there. And shouldn't you take all the children outside so they can get some fresh air?"

You have to begin by seeing, talking with, listening to, and learning from the people who are in the field, day in and day out.

At that moment I realized how often people, even with the best intentions, observe teachers and classrooms, then give feedback without knowing a big part of the story—what is happening and why. Life in a classroom is complicated. This woman's tone (her nice clothes, too, I have to admit) left me feeling defensive and annoyed. In fact, it was another week before I tried out her idea about moving the water table and found she was right.

She came into my classroom with knowledge about high-quality infant and toddler programs and environments but without seeing me as a thinker and decision maker. How different it would have been if she had said, "I wondered why only two children went outside" or "How do things go at the water table? Have you ever thought about trying ____?"

Yet she provided a great insight that I have since applied to my work of writing and coaching: You have to begin by seeing, talking with, listening to, and learning from the people who are in the field, day in and day out. It is the first and most important step in supporting them as professionals who can make a positive difference for young children. Without this person-to-person connection, chances are that water table is going to stay right where it is.

Shaun: Since 1996 I've worked at Murray Hill Studios doing every job possible in television production. Recently I became an owner along with my friend and mentor,
Marc Wein.

Through Marc's mentorship, I learned a great deal about how to film in an active classroom setting—how to watch, listen, and understand (and, therefore, articulate through videos)—the many levels of learning and discovery that exist in a classroom. As my interest in early childhood grew, I continued to absorb more and more information with every project. Several projects later, I met Judy, who would also strongly influence my evolution as an early education video producer.

Since our earliest collaborations, my colleagues, who expanded to include Charlotte Stetson and Amy, and I have used video in a unique and pioneering way. Our days are often structured with morning filming sessions in the classroom followed by afternoon interviews with the educators we filmed. Our methods evolved into what is now the common practice of showing the classroom footage to

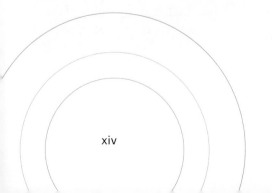

the teacher before the interview. This allows us to ask important, relevant questions about the interactions we filmed. The interview also lets us capture the teacher's observations and reactions to classroom interactions the teacher notices in the video.

In the broadcast industry, this is called "media training." In sports, it's called an "instant replay." But when we actively involve educators in the act of "seeing" what we as coaches and producers see, we create an essential and valuable conduit for professional development.

Like a lot of people, I absolutely despise seeing myself on video. Thoughts of weight loss plans, haircuts, and bad posture flood my mind. The best advice I have is to just get over it. Once you get over the self-consciousness, a kind of clarity sets in that allows you to see the things you are already doing well. This is the most important part. You see things differently when you watch what you've done. Once you focus on your strengths, you can ask the important questions: What am I doing well? How can I continue to use that strength in all aspects of what I do?

Throughout our experiences of filming teachers and coaches, we have witnessed many of their epiphanies. Whether it is through informal, conversational interviews or by showing video clips of classroom interactions, the teachers, coaches, and other professionals we have had the pleasure of working with all comment on the sudden boost of energy and inspiration they feel after working with us. We hope that by reading this book and through watching and listening to the stories and impressions of your colleagues in the field, you will be energized and inspired.

Welcome

WELCOME TO A CONVERSATION ABOUT THE POWERFUL INTERACTIONS APPROACH TO COACHING.

This guide is for you if are a master teacher or coach, coach supervisor, program director, or principal. You may work in a community-based organization, an early education center, an Early Head Start or Head Start program, or a preschool, kindergarten, or early elementary classroom, or you may be a home visitor. You are our colleagues who support teachers with the goal of enhancing the well-being and learning of young children.

Although the guide's focus is on the learning partnership between a coach and a teacher, we believe that coaching with Powerful Interactions will enhance all coaching relationships. To a large extent, the culture or climate of programs and organizations is defined by the interactions among the people who work there. When the quality of interactions improves, human relationships grow deeper and stronger. Positive relationships are a necessary ingredient for learning and can impact the culture and climate, making everyone more open to change and growth. This effect ripples through all organizational roles and levels, ultimately reaching teachers and the central focus—the children.

Michael talks about how interactions between adults benefit children. Video #1. Go to powerfulinteractions.com/coachingbook to access this video. See page 9 for information about how to view the videos in this book plus bonus material.

What Is Coaching?

According to the Colorado Coaching Consortium (2009, 2):

> Coaching is a learning process based on a collaborative relationship that is intentionally designed to promote sustainable growth in the necessary attitudes, skills, and knowledge to effectively implement the best practices for the development of young children and their families.

We have chosen to rely on this definition of coaching because we believe that collaborative relationships and ongoing observation and conversation are central to the success of coaching. At the core of our work is a deep appreciation for teachers whose decisions enhance the quality of programs for children and families.

As Roland Barth, founding director of the Principals' Center at Harvard University, asserts: "Relationships among educators within a school range from vigorously healthy to dangerously competitive. Strengthen those relationships, and you improve professional practice" (2006).

In fact, most studies show that coaching leads to improvements in instructional capacity. For instance, teachers who work with coaches apply their learning more deeply, frequently, and consistently than teachers working alone. Teachers who have coaches improve their capacity to reflect; and they apply their learning not only to their work with children, but also to their work with each other (Kissel et al. 2011).

Yet all too often in many early childhood settings, professional development and assessment of adults is characterized as the coach

- Trying to "fix" teachers' deficits
- Holding the power and knowledge

And sometimes the teacher and the coach are caught up in their own interactions and overwhelmed with too much to accomplish in too little time, unintentionally losing sight of the impact their mood and actions have on children.

We believe this is not by intent. Rather we suspect this is the result of busy people working hard with limited time and resources and operating on automatic pilot with the best intentions of trying to make things better for children.

What Is Coaching with Powerful Interactions?

Coaching with Powerful Interactions identifies and builds on the teacher's strengths to promote that teacher's learning and create positive change in practice.

Powerful Interactions coaching begins with you, the coach. Throughout each day, you have dozens of interactions. Your attitudes about your colleagues and the work you do, and

> Coaching with Powerful Interactions describes an attitude and a way of thinking that can enhance your work. You can use it as a separate coaching model or to complement the coaching model you are already using.

the feelings and emotions you experience and convey, impact the people with whom you interact. Here are a two examples:

A coach, like a travel agent, supports a teacher on his or her journey. Video #2. Go to powerfulinteractions.com/coachingbook to access this video.

- You might be extremely enthusiastic about pretend play with toddlers. For Ms. Tan, your enthusiasm may be inspirational. However, for Mr. Katz, who is quieter and needs an invitation to connect and express himself, it might be overwhelming. He might find it difficult to share questions or doubts about the kitchen area he has set up in his room and his abilities to deepen children's play and learning as they pretend.

- When you truly believe that Ms. Brickley can build a stronger partnership with Leo's (age 4) grandmother, who can be quite demanding, you convey this to Ms. Brickley in a myriad of ways—some conscious and some not. Your actions and words, the expressions on your face, even your posture and the sound of your voice are shaped by your attitude. This supports her efforts, increasing her chances of success.

What you say and do and how you interact with others has a ripple effect that is felt by teachers and young children. In other words, like a stone thrown gently into a pond, your interactions eventually influence teacher practices and, consequently, children's development and learning.

Imagine the dramatic play areas in Ms. Tan's room and Mr. Katz's room. Chances are the toddlers taught by Ms. Tan are engaged with her in activities like pretending to flip pancakes and taking care of sick animals and dolls. In Mr. Katz's room the pretend play area may be quieter. Children may play awhile then move on, perhaps to the art area where they often find Mr. Katz, who paints as a hobby and wants children to enjoy the arts too.

Put yourself in Ms. Brickley's place as she prepares to have a conference with Leo's grandmother, who has been taking care of him since his mother was deployed. After a supportive conversation with her coach, Ms. Brickley finds herself thinking, "I might be a little demanding, too, if my life changed suddenly and I was going to take care of a preschooler for eight months." Even before the two meet, their relationship and work together to support Leo has taken a positive turn.

What you say and do matters. We'll revisit this idea.

Instead of a formula, recipe, or prescribed technique to follow, coaching with Powerful Interactions shows you how to transform everyday interactions into Powerful Interactions. It will help you individualize interactions with teachers to reflect your personal style and the unique blend of strengths, interests, and needs of the teachers you are coaching.

Your Coaching Stance

Your attitude and perspective, and how you perceive and understand interactions, make up your coaching stance. Coaching with Powerful Interactions begins with you and the beliefs and values you bring to your work. Let's briefly explore the beliefs and values that are central to your stance when coaching with Powerful Interactions. Each idea is examined in depth in Chapter 2.

Strengths-based practice was first codified and promoted by Dennis Saleebey and colleagues from the University of Kansas. Saleebey writes, "A strengths-based approach honors a person's capacity to learn, grow and change" (Saleebey 1997, 99). When you visit a classroom, your attitude, therefore, is "I will see strengths. I just need to look for them."

- Do you articulate—or offer clear descriptions of what a teacher does well and talk about why these teaching behaviors support children's well-being and learning—so the teacher can use these behaviors more often and build on them? Or are you more likely to tell a teacher what to do?

- Do you individualize your interactions with a teacher to fit her learning style, strengths, interests, and needs? Or do you have a more standard way of proceeding with your work?

- Do you see yourself as a learning partner with teachers? Are you able and willing to listen and learn, to say, "I don't know. Let's figure it out together"? Or do you feel more comfortable and are more likely to assume the role of expert?

- Do you use yourself as your own best resource, modeling for a teacher what to do and how to do it through your words and actions? Or are you more likely to assume the role of telling a teacher how to be and then guiding her behavior?

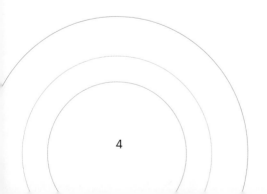

Not About a Score

Although coaching with Powerful Interactions is not about a score, many individuals have told us that using it with teachers often leads to higher scores on standardized program and classroom assessments.

Coaching with Powerful Interactions

It's All About the Children

Have you ever been in a conversation or at a meeting where—no matter the original intent—personalities, politics, territory, or competition for funding or accolades ends up shaping the agenda implicitly or explicitly?

We have been part of many such exchanges, sometimes as participants, other times as facilitators. At one such meeting, a colleague and now friend, Susan Jacobs, executive director of the Association for Supportive Child Care (ASCC) in Arizona, reminded us: It's all about the children. No matter our role, how we dress for work (in jeans and T-shirts or business attire), how we spend our days (on the floor with children, visiting classrooms, or meeting with state leaders to discuss policies), we share a common goal: enhancing the well-being and learning of young children.

In every situation, what you decide to do and say—and how you do and say it—matters. If you are intentional as a coach, work with teachers to arrive at mutually agreed-upon goals, and both share with teachers and take personally the responsibility and accountability for meeting those goals, you can make a positive difference in the lives of young children.

It's Simple and Affordable, and Applies to All of Us

There are three steps to the Powerful Interactions coaching approach. Anyone can learn how to use them. Most of us do some of them already. Implementing them with intentionality takes practice, and that's where we can each continue to learn and grow.

Adopting a coaching approach that is based on Powerful Interactions does not require costly materials or extra funding. This coaching approach provides a shared way of being and a "common language" that can make connections and conversations possible among colleagues and partners, whether at the classroom, program, or state level.

Thanks to Ginger Sandweg, senior director of early learning at First Things First in Arizona, for articulating these ideas so clearly as she opened a meeting.

Coaching Is About Relationships

Whether we are 6 months or 60 years old, meaningful learning takes place in the context of a significant relationship. This is why coaching is about relationships. Learning, growing, and positive change are most likely to occur when a coach and teacher connect, work together to identify goals, share ideas and resources, raise questions, determine next and realistic steps, and support one another over time.

Our work with Powerful Interactions continues to lead us to new and significant relationships. Many colleagues around the country have joined us to articulate and share how to coach using Powerful Interactions. You will hear from many of them on these pages and in the videos in this guide. The following are a few of the colleagues who have shared their experiences:

 Diana Courson is the associate director of Arkansas State University Childhood Services, where she teaches about coaching and supervises early childhood (birth through age 5) coaches in Arkansas.

 Irene Garneau is an instructional specialist at Wintonbury Early Childhood Magnet School, a public early childhood inclusion program in Bloomfield, Connecticut, serving children age 3 through kindergarten.

 Tychawn Johnson is a coach for preschool teachers in a public school district in Jersey City, New Jersey.

 Sarah Leibert is a first-year coach of kindergarten teachers at Wintonbury Magnet School.

Michael Luft is the associate director of the Ben Samuels Child Development Center of Montclair State University. This program serves infants and toddlers through preschool, with a full inclusion model.

Helena Pereira is a coach in Asbury Park, New Jersey, where she specializes in supporting dual language learners who are 3 and 4 years old.

Thoughts About Coaching with Powerful Interactions

Coaching with Powerful Interactions is a conversation about the practice of coaching. We invite you to consider that what you say and do as a coach matters—to teachers and ultimately to young children and their families. Applying insights and strategies about coaching that you learn will enhance your effectiveness no matter what coaching approach or model you may be using, no matter the setting where you practice.

Chapter 1 looks at the three steps of a Powerful Interaction that allow you to intentionally connect with a teacher and to extend learning to reach a desired outcome: Be Present, Connect, and Extend Learning.

Chapter 2 invites you to consider your coaching stance or how your beliefs, attitude, and perspective about teaching, learning, and coaching shape your decisions as you coach with Powerful Interactions.

Chapter 3 looks at what you do as you are present, connect, and extend learning in your work with a teacher.

Throughout this guide, you will find helpful insights, strategies, opportunities to reflect, tips for handling time issues and reality checks to keep the conversation grounded in the lives of coaches. In the words and in the video clips in this guide, you will find the voices of other coaches as they share insights and model aspects of coaching with Powerful Interactions.

This guide can help you to

- Develop a coaching stance and way of being if you are a new coach or are working with new coaches
- Reflect upon your stance and your coaching practice
- Refuel your energy and remind you of the importance of your work
- Step back from a challenging situation, take a breath, and approach the situation with a new perspective and new ideas about how to move forward

We hope it is a guide you will return to often, on your own and in conversation with colleagues. Like you, we continue to learn about coaching with Powerful Interactions.

We invite you to pause, take a breath, and join the conversation.

Judy, Amy, and Shaun

Video Clips in This Book

NOTE: Congratulations! Because you purchased this book, you can access all these video clips and other bonus material by using the QR code or at powerfulinteractions.com/coachingbook

Chapter

Powerful Interactions Between Coach and Teacher: An Introduction

Interactions are the exchanges in words and gestures that you have with teachers (and others) every day. Yet too often, as we know from coaches across the country and our own experiences, interactions might occur on autopilot or in the midst of multitasking. As a result, the interactions can deplete people's energy and sense of effectiveness and undermine the goal of enhancing children's well-being and learning. Consider the example on the next page from the perspectives of the coach and the teacher.

You begin a Powerful Interaction when you pause to think and to decide how best to proceed.

Quinn is a coach. He just received an email from his supervisor saying she needs to talk with him as soon as possible. About what he has no idea. The end-of-the-month reports are due tomorrow and Quinn was planning to spend the morning working on them. There's a knock on his door. It's Jasmine, a teacher who is looking for a copy of an article that he shared with her a few days ago. He can tell she also would like to sit and talk a few minutes. He says, "Are you sure that article isn't somewhere in all the papers on your shelf? If you can't find it, I'll email it to you this afternoon."

What if you were Jasmine? She reached out for information and support, but walked away feeling that not only have her organizational skills been questioned, but her needs were not seen or, worse, were ignored.

Now imagine what the result might be if Quinn's interactions with Jasmine and other teachers were more intentional? In other words, what if he had the opportunity to pause and think about what to say or do—and how—then moved forward? Enter coaching with Powerful Interactions.

What Is a Powerful Interaction Between a Coach and Teacher?

The three steps of a Powerful Interaction—Be Present, Connect, and Extend Learning—serve as your frame. Following each step in turn allows you to intentionally connect with a teacher and extend learning to reach a desired outcome. For example, the focus might be having conversations with children or being able to delegate in the classroom. The outcome is something you have both agreed is necessary and beneficial.

Using Powerful Interactions as your coaching frame supports you in both beginning and developing a strong, trusting relationship between you and the teacher you are coaching. Such relationships are prerequisites for learning and sustained positive change in a teacher's practice. Having a Powerful Interaction with a teacher can begin the development of a sense of trust between the two of you. Over time, continuing to have Powerful Interactions sustains that trust.

You begin a Powerful Interaction when you pause to think and to decide how best to proceed. To continue a Powerful Interaction with a teacher, you make a conscious decision to connect in a personal way. For example, after observing for a while you might say, "I see you talking with Adrian about the names of insects. I'm interested in hearing about your goals for this conversation with Adrian, and I want to learn more about what you are thinking and doing."

Your decision to share your curiosity and phrase your comments as an invitation for the teacher to share more about her practice creates a connection. Over time, connections like this develop into trust and help to reduce the sense of isolation and stress so common among teachers of young children. Your trusting relationship opens the door to a partnership to extend learning about practice and young children.

Shante, a teaching assistant in an inclusion classroom of 3-year-olds, and Irene, Shante's coach, have known each other for several years. Shante's goal is to individualize her interactions with children. During a scheduled classroom visit, Irene observed Shante interacting with Ethan during center time. As you watch the conversation in the video, notice how Irene offers feedback to Shante and invites her to think about how she can use interactions to document Ethan's thinking and learning, information Shante needs in order to individualize.

Shante and Irene have a coaching conversation. Video #3. Go to powerfulinteractions.com/coachingbook to access this video, the other videos in this book, and bonus material.

Three steps can turn everyday coaching interactions into Powerful Interactions. We look briefly at each one:

Step One: Be Present to Coach

To Be Present means having an "inner quiet," allowing you to think and make decisions about what to say and do with maximum clarity and effectiveness. This is the core of intentionality.

Intentionality

Thinking and making decisions about what to say and do with maximum clarity and effectiveness. This is the core of intentionality. For example, when you are present in the moment with an inner quiet, you can be deliberate, purposeful, and thoughtful as you decide what to say and do in your coaching interactions with a teacher.

Tychawn offers insights about static.
Video #4. Go to powerfulinteractions.com/coachingbook to access this video.

Static

The internal "noise" in your mind when there are so many things going on that you cannot focus on just one thing. Static interferes with being able to listen, to think, or to question. The first step of a Powerful Interaction, Be Present, helps quiet the static so you can think and make decisions about what to say and do.

Ever feel like there's so much going on in your mind you can't focus on just one thing? We call this noise static. It's like the annoying crackling sound when there's interference on your phone and you can't hear your friend tell you what time and where to meet. Static can drive you crazy!

In a quiet, static-free space, you can be mindful about what is going on inside of yourself and around you. You can pay attention "on purpose, in the present moment, and nonjudgmentally, to the unfolding of experience moment to moment" (Kabat-Zinn 2003, 145).

Being Present Leads to More Effective Coaching

When you are present, you can pay attention to another person and connect with him or her. This allows you to decide how best to respond to this person, in this moment, and at the same time, to move your work together forward.

Practice intentionality. When you are present in the moment with an inner quiet, you can be deliberate, purposeful, and thoughtful (Epstein 2014) as you decide what to say and do in your coaching interactions with a teacher.

You are freed from thoughts and feelings of past exchanges and future experiences, plans, or expectations that can lead you to operate in autopilot mode. You can take a breath, put your judgments on hold, listen, and reflect on the many facets of a situation. This makes your thinking clearer, opens the door to new possibilities for how you might respond, and makes it possible to be open and engage with a mindset of curiosity and acceptance (Broderick 2013).

Draw on your strengths and use yourself as your own best resource. When the static in your head quiets, you can draw upon the strengths you bring to your practice. These may include

- Your unique way of being and engaging
- What you know about the person you are working with
- Your knowledge and skills around communicating effectively and supporting another adult's learning and professional development

Pause for a moment to observe yourself and the teacher. Interactions are filled with meanings for everyone. Everything you do—your smile or still face, the tone of your voice, whether you are relaxed or exuding tension—and everything you say engages the personality, beliefs, likes, and dislikes of the person you are interacting with (Pawl & Dombro 2004).

When you are present, you can observe yourself and others. Whether during a planned coaching session or an informal hallway exchange with a teacher, pausing for a moment or two to pay attention and become more aware of the impact that you have on others and that they have on you allows you to respond rather than react. By being present, you can interact thoughtfully and as usefully as possible.

Be mindful and adopt and create a positive mindset. The more you can focus on the positive, the more positive your interactions and results will be (Langer 2009).

The challenges of being both supervisor and coach. Video #5. Go to powerfulinteractions.com/coachingbook to access this video.

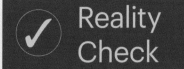

Step Two: Connecting as a Coach

Most people in our field would say they are good at "connecting with others and building relationships," and in many cases they are. Yet all too often it stops there. A Powerful Interactions coach goes beyond connecting and building relationships to "using" relationships intentionally to extend a teacher's learning. When you use the Powerful Interaction approach, you convey to the person you are coaching, "I notice you, I'm interested in you, and I want to get to know you even better." This moment of personal connection deepens the trusting relationship growing between you.

Connecting and Trusting Relationships Lead to More Effective Coaching

As you and the teacher you are coaching jointly build a trusting relationship, the teacher is likely to feel safe, supported, and nurtured. Feeling this way, she may be open to taking risks, sharing practices, and trying new approaches (Tschannen-Moran & Tschannen-Moran 2011b).

Sometimes we talk about relationships as if they are a task that can be completed and checked off a "to do" list, freeing us to turn our attention to the "real" job of coaching. For an effective coach, connecting to build relationships is an ongoing, necessary part of promoting and supporting a teacher's learning.

After thinking about relationships in this way, Morgan, a coach from New Jersey, shared this insight:

> I set aside time for paperwork, meetings, and more meetings. But after the beginning of the year I never think about taking time to focus on relationship building, which is what lets me be effective. I'm going to start writing relationships at the top of my calendar every month to remind me to focus on them all year long.

Step Three: Coaching to Extend Learning

It's easy to enter a teacher's classroom and tell her what to do or offer a fix. We've all done it. Perhaps you've rearranged some furniture or the dramatic play area. You might have felt effective for a minute or two, but chances are your "fix" didn't stick.

With Powerful Interactions coaching, coaches and teachers collaborate as learners to create meaningful change. When coaches extend learning, they make sensitive and responsive decisions about what to say and do in the moment to help a teacher move her learning and practice forward. To do so effectively, a coach must be open to learning with and from a teacher, even as the coach offers a rich array of experiences, information, strategies, and insights.

Coaching to extend learning includes helping a teacher put goals into words, then breaking goals into clear and achievable steps. It means pointing out moments of effectiveness as the teacher moves toward her goal and describing why her actions and words matter to children. It means inviting her to think about her intentional decision making.

In this way the teacher can acknowledge, repeat, and build on her strengths. She can become a more intentional decision maker, able to apply and adapt what she has learned day by day, during, between, and after her work with you.

Extending Learning and Continuing to Learn Lead to More Effective Coaching

Engaging in a learning partnership as Irene did with Shante in the video described on page 13 can free both coach and teacher from feeling like they have to figure things out alone. Learning together allows both the teacher and the coach to say, "I'm not sure" and opens the door to looking for and discovering answers and possibilities together.

As a coach in a learning partnership, you can keep the focus of your interactions on shared goals. Many coaches have described times they enter into a conversation with a teacher and slip into therapist mode as they listen to a teacher's personal problems or problems at work. While these conversations sometimes strengthen the coach–teacher

Continuing to Learn

The quote that follows describes the quandary of having to support a teacher in a situation with which the coach is unfamiliar. As recent research has revealed, classroom interactions in which teachers intentionally promote learning are few and far between (Early et al. 2005; Pianta 2010).

"It has been a long time since I've been in the classroom. How am I supposed to help a teacher with transitions if I'm not sure how to do it? It often looks like total confusion to me as she helps the group get out the door."

If Jillian's words resonate for you, you're not alone. It is a sentiment we hear frequently. We believe that recognizing and articulating what you don't know allows you to extend your own learning. The coaching strategies outlined in this chapter are a good place to begin.

Reality Check

While the steps of a Powerful Interaction are the same regardless of the ages of the players, there are differences in interactions between children and adults and between adults and adults. Note the wisdom of our colleague, Monica Vacca:

"Due to their life experiences, adults have more insecurities and worries and reasons to be defensive when approaching a coaching relationship than children do. What adults bring in terms of their background, culture, values, work ethics and habits, and professional and adult learning experiences as well as life experiences can color the interaction. These factors can also influence the interaction's power for either the positive or the negative. Adults are more likely to be quick to develop first impressions, and to be not so quick to get beyond them (as a result of life experiences, etc.). Adults, and teachers in particular, are likely to bring more static to interactions than children do simply because of all that is on their plates (in most cases it's too much!). An adult's **approach** to interactions is more affected by or colored by their years of experience with their profession and with other people in all areas of life and by their own static. Adults are more articulate about their thoughts and the messages they want to convey. They are also cognitively capable of deeper reflection."

relationship, coaches tell us they actually feel frustrated at not accomplishing concrete goals. Being a learning partner makes it easier to listen for a few minutes, acknowledge what is going on, and then say, "This is our time to continue our work around _____ ."

The Three Steps: A Cumulative Effect

Often we think about steps as being followed one after the other and checked off as "done" when each one occurs. It is different with the three steps of coaching with Powerful Interactions because the steps are sequential and cumulative.

You begin with step 1 by pausing to be present. In this frame of mind, you can decide to add step 2, choosing what to say and do to connect with the teacher you are coaching. Staying present and connected, you then add step 3 as you identify a way to extend the mutual learning partnership. Yet even as three steps build upon each other during a single interaction, they are creating a history of Powerful Interactions that will help make future interactions even more powerful.

In Chapter 3, we describe each step in detail to help you understand the importance of each one. Yet in real life, as your coaching interactions unfold, the steps are apt to happen very quickly. Before we get to Chapter 3, however, we describe the five principles that guide the Powerful Interactions coaching stance in Chapter 2.

2 Chapter

Coaching with Powerful Interactions: Five Principles

Powerful Interactions coaching begins with **you**—**how** you act and **how** you approach coaching. The beliefs, attitudes, and perspective about teaching, coaching, and learning that you bring to your work is what we call your coaching stance.

Donald Schön, who wrote the seminal book *The Reflective Practitioner*, states that stance "involves not only attitudes and feelings, but ways of perceiving and understanding" (1987, 119). Your coaching stance affects how you use the three steps of Powerful Interactions in your coaching.

In Chapter 3 we take a closer look at the three steps of coaching with Powerful Interactions: the **"what"** you do.

Five principles guide the Powerful Interactions coaching stance.

1. A strengths-based perspective searches for and highlights competence. Coaches observe teachers with the intent of finding teachers' moments of effectiveness.

2. Articulation—sharing observations and describing why they are important—allows the person to repeat the action with greater intentionality. Coaches observe teachers' practice, clearly and accurately describing it and the impact it has on children's learning so teachers can use the information to improve their practice.

3. Individualizing supports the development of respectful, trusting relationships needed for learning. Coaches tailor what they say and do to find the "just right fit" in their work with teachers.

4. A mutual learning partnership promotes shared responsibility and accountability. Coaches and teachers develop a shared plan for change that is meaningful and sustainable.

5. Modeling matters: what you say and do influences all outcomes. Coaches model attitudes and behaviors that support relationships and learning in everything they do and say in their partnerships with teachers. They hope that teachers will apply these attitudes and behaviors in their work with children and families.

As you will see, the principles overlap and relate to each other. We have pulled them apart to explain them—to highlight how important each principle is to your effectiveness as a coach.

Some of these principles may be very familiar to you and part of who you are as coach. Others may be less familiar.

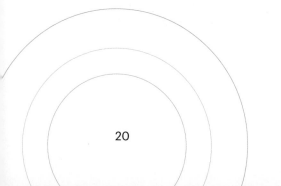

Stance

How you act and how you approach your work as coach, including how you perceive and understand interactions is your coaching stance. It begins with you and the beliefs and values you bring to your work. This is the cascading or parallel process of how coach-to-teacher interactions shape the quality of what happens between teachers and children. For example, how you interact with a coach models how a teacher can interact with children.

Strengths-Based

A strengths-based perspective begins by looking for effective practice. Adult learners want to be validated for what they already know, recognized for their strengths and experience. For example, when coaching with Powerful Interactions, you enter a classroom with the attitude that you will see a teacher's strengths even if his or her strengths might not be immediately apparent. This attitude builds on a teacher's strengths with the intention of creating positive change in his or her practice.

Articulation

Sharing observations and describing why they are important, providing information that teachers can use intentionally. For example, as a coach you observe a teacher's practice and objectively and accurately describe it to the teacher and how the teacher's actions impact children's learning so he or she can use the information to use this practice with greater intentionality in the future.

Individualizing

In coaching individualizing means finding the "just right fit" that supports your work with a teacher. For example, as a coach you might tailor what you say and do to find the "just right fit" in your work with teachers. This might include your posture, tone of voice, the carefully crafted questions you ask, and the communication style and mode you use with a teacher.

Ripples of Change

Your coaching stance, or **how** you act and **how** you approach your work as coach, reflects your beliefs about how teachers learn and interact with children. This is the cascading or parallel process of how coach-to-teacher interactions shape the quality of what happens between teachers and children.

Diana explains how her stance as a coach has evolved. Video #6. Go to powerfulinteractions.com/coachingbook to access this video, the other videos in this book, and bonus material.

We invite you to join us in having a willingness to continually examine our practice as educators. In this way we can foster coaching relationships with teachers that lead to quality enhancements.

Examining and evolving your stance is part of being an ongoing, engaged learner. It requires confidence and trust to let yourself pause a moment to think about what you do and why, to raise questions, admit mistakes, and be open about aspects of your practice that could be improved. It means that you are comfortable with the idea that often there is not one right answer. It takes the willingness to stumble as you engage in course corrections.

We have done our share of stumbling and evolving as we have used Powerful Interactions for coaching. One thing we've learned: applying these principles in your practice and assuming a Powerful Interactions stance is not a panacea. There will be times when static prevails; we guarantee it.

At the same time, we are certain that the five principles described in this chapter will affect your practice in a way that allows you and the teachers you coach to experience success. With this coaching stance, you invite teachers to join you even as you reduce resistance. (Remember what the consultant said about the placement of the water table in Amy's classroom?) By working together you maximize the possibilities of creating lasting and positive change for the teachers you coach and, ultimately, of effective learning for the children they teach.

Principle One: A Strengths-Based Perspective Searches for and Highlights Competence

Coaches who observe teachers at work with the intent of finding teachers' moments of effectiveness are said to be strengths based. A moment of effectiveness is a specific teaching behavior that positively impacts children's learning. Examples include

- Using a song to ensure a smooth transition from one activity to the next
- Labeling the steps for hand washing with pictures and words—in Spanish and in English—so all of the children can learn this routine and complete it independently

- Sitting at the child's eye level to have a conversation so that the child knows the adult is interested in her and can help her feel safe and comfortable

When using a strengths-based perspective, coaches can identify examples of the teacher's competence to use as the foundation for extending learning. For example, "Several times this morning I noticed you standing next to the slide's ladder, and this supports children's learning by letting them know you are confident in their abilities but are also available should they want to ask for support."

As coach, you are a teacher's mirror, calling attention to moments of effectiveness. You state the facts, without judgment, and then offer a clear statement about why what the teacher did and said in that moment is important and how it impacts a child's learning. For example, "Jo Won, I noticed that you hung photos of the babies and toddlers with their families just above the carpeted climber. That lets them feel connected to and comforted by seeing and touching the people they love most."

Ripples of Change

Searching for a teacher's competence and calling attention to it validates her, and that, in turn, builds trust between you, strengthening your relationship. How you coach a teacher, whether finding strengths or deficits, will likely influence how she "coaches" children.

To establish a respectful working partnership, Tychawn helps a teacher see her own strengths. Video #7. Go to powerfulinteractions.com/coachingbook to access this video.

By calling attention to effective decisions, you validate the teacher and simultaneously empower her to use these teaching actions with greater intentionality.

Often coaches, ourselves included, enter a classroom with the best intent of looking for strengths. Instead, we get off track and spend time noticing deficits to fix. Sandy shares an insight about a shift in her coaching stance:

> Before I was introduced to Powerful Interactions coaching, I was tallying up deficits and trying to fix some of them. I would offer one or two positives to placate people. That seems so shallow now. For me, my shift has been from giving feedback in the Sandy-knows-it-all stance to a strengths-based stance—looking at what a teacher is trying to accomplish and how effective she is at it. Having Powerful Interactions with adults means pausing and putting my agenda aside, which has made this shift possible. We want to work with teachers in the same way as we want them to be with children.

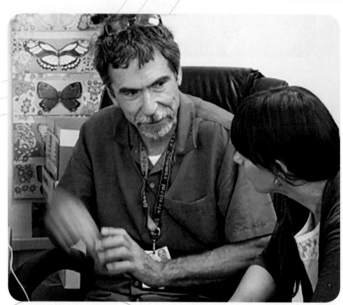

As Sandy described, strengths-based coaching requires a shift in mindset from looking to correct deficits to acknowledging that everyone has strengths. It means being optimistic about possibilities for change. As Saleebey describes it: "Strengths-based coaching is an approach honoring the innate wisdom of the human spirit, the inherent capacity for transformation" (Saleebey 2013, 1).

To this Diana adds:

> A strengths-based approach to coaching is different from making positive comments or being nice. Highlighting a person's strengths (even when they are simply first steps towards a goal) encourages him to use those strengths more frequently and in a variety of situations. In this way you increase the person's self-efficacy, and that in turn empowers the person to take another step on his professional growth journey. Taking a strengths-based approach is learning to see the seeds of growth that have already been planted in the person's practice and are ready to be nurtured.

Coaching with Powerful Interactions

A Strengths-Based Perspective Makes You a More Effective Coach

Research on adults and motivation explains that when people feel judged they may become angry, fearful, or anxious (Chao 2009). These emotions can cause a great deal of static that interferes with being able to listen, to think, and to question.

When you adopt a strengths-based stance, you quiet this emotional static, making it possible for you to invite teachers to explore their practice with you. As you highlight moments of effectiveness, you help teachers to build self-efficacy, set self-directed learning goals, brainstorm strategies, and design ways of moving forward. Teachers can use their strengths to transform their weaknesses (Tschannen-Moran & Tschannen-Moran 2011a). The paradigm of professional development shifts from "I am the expert training you" to "Let's have a conversation about your strengths and how you can use them to be even more effective."

A Strengths-Based Perspective in Practice

What does a strengths-based perspective look like in action? It begins when a coach enters a classroom looking for effective practice. Clarissa Wallace, an early childhood coach in Arkansas, uses this metaphor:

> I imagine myself to be a yellow highlighter in the teacher's classroom, highlighting what she is doing effectively so that she can do it over and over again.

Let's read how Joan applies the strengths-based approach when coaching Randy, a veteran preschool teacher who works with 4-year-olds. In this scenario, Joan quiets her static, observes and finds moments when Randy is effective, then highlights her strengths in preparation to work with Randy to build on them:

> Joan is visiting Randy's classroom for the first time during learning center time. Joan has heard from previous coaches that Randy's voice often dominates the classroom.

Joan thinks:

Wow! I see what her previous coaches meant. Her voice is loud, and the expression on her face seems annoyed. Talk about static! This makes me nuts. The climate of this classroom feels harsh and cold. Yet the teaching assistant's voice is so absolutely quiet. Okay, I have to wait and watch to see if there's a moment when Randy is a bit quieter or more relaxed.

After 25 minutes, Randy joins 4-year-olds Janelle and Rowan in dramatic play. As she sits down at the table, she asks in a friendly, quieter tone: "What's for lunch? It smells delicious. May I join you?" Both children scurry to get her some food and they continue to chat for about two or three minutes.

Joan thinks:

Here's a moment when Randy is being effective. She's using a quieter voice and she's sitting at the children's eye level. She's engaging in back and forth conversation with them. The children respond by telling her what they are cooking, offering her food, and putting a fork and plate for her on the table.

Joan watches for a few more minutes and then steps out of the classroom to prepare her written feedback.

Joan used a Powerful Interactions approach to focus on Randy's strengths. She documents Randy's strengths so that she can reflect them back to her. Writing and sharing observations and thoughts about the effect of the teacher's practice helps the teacher see and recognize what she says and does and why it matters to children's development. Teachers need this information to appreciate the impact and importance of the decisions they make and become more intentional. The process encourages teachers to do more of what works to support children's well-being and learning. (You will read more about Joan's feedback to Randy on p. 30.)

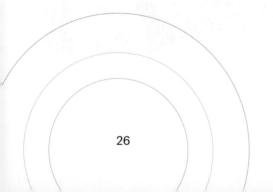

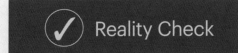

It all sounds good, you might say, but what happens when I have a concern about what a teacher says or does? The response depends on the nature of the concern. If the concern is obvious or a safety hazard, such as poisons stored on the counter instead of in a locked cabinet or children without appropriate supervision, address it in a direct and respectful manner. In this example, Ms. Kate, a program director, addresses an issue she noticed—an outdoor playtime with poor supervision. There were 15 children outdoors, two teachers with 10 children in the garden and five children playing in the sand area without adult supervision. Ms. Kate made a conscious decision not to jump in and correct the teachers—Mr. Reynolds and Ms. Jackson, the assistant teacher— publicly. Instead she remained outside, supervising and engaging with the unattended children in the sand area. Upon returning to her office she took a breath and sent an email to Mr. Reynolds, the lead teacher. She said that she wanted to talk with him about outdoor play and that they could do so during his afternoon prep period. He responded immediately and they arranged for a 20-minute conversation at 1:00. Here's how it went:

Mr. Reynolds: Hi, you wanted to see me?

Ms. Kate: Yes. Thanks for stopping by in the middle of your prep. I know you're busy. How are you doing?

Mr. Reynolds: Good. Thanks.

Ms. Kate: I noticed on the playground this morning that you and your assistant were in the garden planting with several children; there was lively conversation and lots of excited learning. I also noticed, however, that quite a few children were playing in the sand area without supervision. I wondered if you had picked up on that.

Mr. Reynolds (sounding defensive): Really? Maybe for a minute. I have to respond to children who ask me questions. I was called over to the planting area.

Ms. Kate: Outdoors can be challenging, especially when many children are busy in one area of the yard. However, ensuring children's safety at all times is paramount. Let's figure out how you and Ms. Jackson can be certain of children's safety at all times. I've noticed at center time you and Ms. Jackson take turns interacting with children and floating around the classroom. Would a system like this work outdoors?

Mr. Reynolds: Yes, we do that.

Ms. Kate: Perhaps during outdoor time you could divide the time for interacting and floating and check in with each other midway through.

Mr. Reynolds: I'll talk to Ms. Jackson.

Ms. Kate: Please let me know toward the end of the week if this is working out for you.

Ms. Kate conveyed her message without attack or judgment. She simply stated the facts. She didn't insist that it was longer than a minute or say, "I stayed outside to supervise for 10 minutes." Her goal was to call his attention to the problem and offer him guidance about what could work to address the concern. And, she'll be scrupulous about checking back later in the week.

Principle Two: Articulation, Sharing Observations and Describing Why They Are Important, Provides Information to Be Used in Intentional Ways

Articulating, putting observations and thoughts about educational practice into words, allows you and teachers to access, reflect upon, clarify, and communicate about them.

Articulation allows a teacher to see and be responsible for her teaching behaviors and to acknowledge that her decisions matter. It is as if a coach's articulation transforms her teaching behaviors into a set of resources she can use with greater purpose or intentionality. Intentionality, "interactions between children and teachers in which teachers purposefully challenge, scaffold, and extend children's skills and have an understanding of expected outcomes of instruction" (Epstein 2014, 242), is the key to creating high-quality learning experiences for children.

The approach outlined in this guide is not about a coach's opinions or preferences. Rather, a Powerful Interactions coach objectively notes a teacher's moments of effectiveness and then adds weight by putting them into words and describing why they matter for children: "I see you have labeled children's cubbies with their names—written in their home languages—and a photo of them with their families. What a powerful way to help children learn name recognition and, at the same time, convey that children and families are important in the classroom community!"

Using Articulation to Promote Intentionality Makes You a More Effective Coach

When you put effective elements of a teacher's practice into specific and clear language, it is as if you put her actions and words on the table. Once they are "visible" you can reflect upon and talk about them. You create common ground for your work together.

As a result, a teacher begins to see herself as a decision maker, which is the first step toward being intentional. Teachers make dozens of decisions every day. Yet our experience is that many teachers forget or don't realize they are decision makers. We wish you could be with us when we talk about decision making with a group of teachers to hear the quiet hum of surprise and amazement that often resonates throughout the room.

As a teacher begins to own her practice and become more consciously competent, her understanding of **what** she does (her practice) and **why** it is important (the theory and outcomes) deepens. Evidence indicates that this can lead teachers to think more deeply about their work, and it can motivate them to explore new ideas and approaches (Anning & Edwards 2006). Ultimately, this leads to teachers strengthening their relationships with children and extending their learning more effectively.

When you use articulation over time, you may find that the teacher's language becomes more clear and specific and that yours does, too.

Articulation in Practice

Think of yourself as a teacher's mirror. You reflect back moments of effectiveness through factual statements, without judgment. Then offer a clear statement about how the teacher's words and/or actions impact a child's learning.

Learning to articulate the "why" is an ongoing professional development conversation for coaches using Powerful Interactions. Video #8. Go to powerfulinteractions.com/coachingbook to access this video.

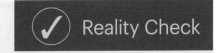

✓ Reality Check

We don't often hear the word *articulation* used in our field. Yet we intentionally decided it to use it in this principle. Why? Articulation goes beyond giving feedback or guiding a teacher's behavior. It promotes clarity in thinking and communicating about practice, creating a common ground for professional development conversations that in turn increases potential for positive change.

Joan, the coach, and Randy, the preschool teacher (see p. 25), agreed that after their first visit, Joan will send feedback in an email. This gives Randy a chance to think about it before they meet again. Here is the email Joan sends:

Hi, Randy,

Thanks for welcoming me into your classroom. I noticed that when you engaged with the two children in dramatic play, you sat with them at the table. By being at their eye level, you show them that you are interested in their play and want to spend time with them. I'm sure you know that's a great way to nurture your relationship with them, because you've seen how the children respond.

I also noticed that you used three different Powerful Interactions Extend Learning strategies to support children's learning. You used a conversational tone of voice as you engaged with the children in "real" conversation about the soup. You got right into their imaginative play, mirroring the story they were beginning to build. And you introduced them to a rich vocabulary word—delicious. The more you sit at children's eye level and talk with them in conversational tones, the more you build a positive climate in your classroom.

I look forward to our next visit. I can come again in two weeks, on Tuesday. Would center time be good for you? And would it be possible for us to use 20 minutes of nap time for a conversation? Thanks again. I look forward to hearing from you.

Joan

Joan articulates Randy's strengths for two reasons. By validating something she does well, Joan begins to establish a trusting relationship with Randy. Moreover, the strength that Joan witnessed in dramatic play is a first step in supporting a change in Randy's practice: helping her use a warmer, quieter tone with children and engaging with them more, not as director of the action but rather as participant in their play.

Articulates

Communicating objective observations, including why what you observed is important, with the purpose of helping a teacher improve his or her practice. For example, as a coach you observe a teacher's practice and objectively and accurately describes it to the teacher so he or she can use the information to improve his or her practice.

Randy's email response affirms for Joan that articulation can lead to a teacher's increased intentionality. Here's how Randy responded:

> Thanks for your email, Joan. After reading what you said, I'm making more of an effort to sit with children in dramatic play and in other centers too. When I sit down with them and have conversations, I'm amazed at how many words they know. Yesterday, Reza, who I thought knew only a few English words, was suddenly telling me all about the menu and letting me know that the special of the day was spaghetti.

Joan's Powerful Interactions coaching stance is developing. It begins with her belief that finding and identifying strengths is the foundation for building competence. To foster Randy's teaching competence, Joan uses articulation to reflect Randy's strengths back to her. This gives Randy information she needs to be more aware of what she does and why: to be more intentional. Yet that information by itself is not enough. To maximize the possibility that the information leads to learning and positive change in practice, it has to be conveyed within a trusting relationship. This leads us to the next principle.

Principle Three: Individualizing Supports the Development of Respectful, Trusting Relationships Needed for Learning

The Powerful Interactions approach to coaching talks about individualizing as finding the "just right fit"— tailoring what you say and do to fit the situation and another person's personality, needs, strengths, cultural and linguistic background, and interests. Are you younger or less experienced than the person you are coaching? Are you the person's supervisor as well as coach? Do you share the teacher's culture or come from a different cultural background?

Every adult is an individual, just as every child is an individual. It takes "getting over yourself" (remember Judy's story?) to be able to focus and give yourself time to get to know the teacher you are coaching. When you take the time to get to know her interests, dreams, personality, and needs, you show respect and build a relationship that is critical to the coaching process.

Ripples of Change

When you use specific and clear language as you articulate what a teacher says and does, you increase the likelihood that she will do the same in her conversations with children. This, in turn, provides information children need to extend their thinking and learning.

Dana, an early childhood supervisor and coach, shares this insight about individualizing:

> I have to know myself as a coach to adjust how I interact with teachers. I'm not a real touchy-feely person. I'm pretty direct. Teachers know that my direct style comes from a place of wanting to help and be supportive. One teacher might be just as direct as I am as we talk about how to change her habit of saying to children: "You're right." Another teacher has a different goal that she is working on and a quiet, gentle style of interacting with children—and with me. To be effective, I have to know each person who works here, their learning and interacting styles, and how to address their particular needs.

Individualizing requires being intentional. The decisions you make about everything, from your posture to your tone of voice to the carefully crafted questions you ask to help teachers extend their thinking, affect your relationship with a teacher and the progress you make in your work together.

When it comes to coaching, one size does not fit all.

Individualizing Makes You a More Effective Coach

Monica Brinkerhoff, a colleague and coach in Arizona, shares this thought:

> I believe that individualizing for children is imperative, and I want to practice this same belief in my work as a coach. By maintaining an attitude of lifelong learning and regularly reflecting on my coaching practice, I can be more purposeful in my efforts to respond to each teacher.

Communicating and establishing trusting relationships with teachers who are trying to change their practice requires being sensitive to their dilemmas, fears, and celebrations (Annenberg Institute for School Reform 2004). When you find the "just right fit," you demonstrate this sensitivity, and trust builds. This allows a teacher to feel safe enough to explore, question, and even stumble with you as you explore her practice together.

By individualizing, you are more likely to be able to talk together about a teacher's concerns and needs in regard to her practice. Research shows that supports for improved teaching and learning are more effective when they are tailored to needs identified by teachers and when the approach to learning is collaborative and inquiry-based (Hsieh et al. 2009).

Individualizing in Practice

We'd like to share a story about how Judy and Amy scrambled to individualize so we could meet the needs of a young teacher and begin to build a trusting coaching relationship.

> We walked into Ms. Shellie's Early Head Start classroom. The goal for Ms. Shellie and the other teachers we would visit that day had been established by program leadership. We planned to introduce ourselves and connect as a first step in beginning six months of working together around having conversations with children.
>
> Upon opening the door we were met by a young teacher with a look of panic in her eyes. She was surrounded by children, most of whom were not engaged in productive play. We looked at one another and decided to excuse ourselves for a moment. Our static was leading to judgments that wouldn't be helpful to our ability to support her. We stepped into the hallway, out of the chaos, to think.
>
> We decided to make this first visit very short. Both of us would use the time to help to calm the environment by connecting with a child demonstrating particularly challenging behavior. And that's what we did.
>
> We also recognized that Ms. Shellie's need for support around positive guidance needed to be our priority. When we asked her about that, we could see her shoulders relax. "Yes," she said. "That's something I need and want to work on."
>
> We made a plan with her to come back in two weeks. During our second visit we searched for strengths. We took photos and videos. As the two of us debriefed to prepare for our conversation with Ms. Shellie, we had a hard time finding a moment, even a sliver, of effectiveness. Then we realized that even though she was struggling to teach a group of children, she was very skilled at connecting with individual young children. Our work together would begin there.

One of the photos we took that day showed her smiling broadly during a circle time dance. In another she is smiling and meeting a child's eyes during a lunchtime conversation. And in another photo she has her arms around a child who was sad after his dad said goodbye.

As she looked at the photos, Ms. Shellie had tears in her eyes. "I get so busy, I never knew I smiled like that, or that children paid so much attention to me."

"I notice children look into your eyes when you smile at them," Judy said. "Your smile is one way of guiding children's behavior."

We agreed to focus together next time on positive guidance strategies. As our conversation ended, she had a huge smile on her face. "Will you send me copies of these photos so I can share them with my dad?" she asked. "They show me being the kind of teacher I want to be."

As we said goodbye, she gave us a hug. Our decision to individualize our plan for working with Ms. Shellie was a first step to forming a trusting relationship with her.

To set the stage for a mutual learning partnership that promotes shared responsibility and accountability, keep these three things in mind:

- Focus on a teacher's strengths
- Use articulation to promote intentionality
- Individualize to build a respectful, trusting relationship necessary for learning

Principle Four: A Mutual Learning Partnership Promotes Shared Responsibility and Accountability

Some coaches have told us that they feel uncomfortable and uncertain when faced with a teacher's question that they are not able to answer. Others describe the opposite experience. Sandy shared an example of learning together with a teacher when a child with fetal alcohol syndrome enrolled in the program in the middle of the year. Teacher and coach sat together at the computer to do some research. They both learned about strategies to use and resources they could obtain to support the child and collaborate with his family.

Being confident and wise enough to say, "I'm not sure, let's find this out together," creates a balance and partnership in the relationship. You and the teacher each have an equal voice as you learn together. You hear one another and learn from each other (Gardner & Toope 2011). Each brings knowledge and competencies to the partnership. Each has much to learn and gain from working with the other. You work together to develop a shared agreement about goals and steps to move forward even when you are not together.

As partners you share the responsibility and accountability for the effectiveness of the work on behalf of children. You are accountable to one another to follow through on your responsibilities and commitments.

In this way, your relationship is a safe and secure environment that supports your collaborative learning and, ultimately, the learning of young children.

Building a Mutual Learning Partnership Makes You a More Effective Coach

When a coach and a teacher create a learning partnership, they avoid the power dynamic that often develops unintentionally in the coaching relationship. You are freed from the constraints of assuming you are the expert, the keeper of the knowledge, and the "fixer" of problems. You bring knowledge and expertise to the relationship, but the teacher brings knowledge too. Remember Amy's story. She knew the whole picture of her classroom, including why certain decisions were made. In a learning partnership, the teacher also is freed—from the common assumption that her role is to listen, learn, and do what you say.

In a partnership the goals of your work as a coach are elevated from solving problems or providing "quick fixes" to creating lasting positive change on behalf of young children. As research on motivation and change tells us, when people feel ownership of the change process, change is more meaningful and more likely to be sustained (Kanter 2012).

A Mutual Learning Partnership in Practice

As in all relationships, there are sometimes missteps or bumps in a coaching partnership. Here is a story about Leila, a coach who is a supervisor of other coaches. She responded to

Ripples of Change

When you and a teacher build a learning partnership and you follow through and do what you say you'll do, she may be more likely to build learning partnerships with children in which both she and the children follow through with responsibilities.

a misstep in a way that deepened her partnership with another coach and promoted their shared responsibility.

Reflections

Take a few moments to think about how you truly feel about the idea of being a partner, rather than the expert or fixer. What's comfortable about this idea? What might unsettle you? If necessary, how might you address your feelings?

I had scheduled a supervision meeting with Margot, another coach. When she showed up, I was not ready. I hadn't taken time to get my mind ready, so static was running high. A dozen different things had distracted me that morning. I have to admit that they continued to do so, even as Margot came into my office and sat down.

I knew I was fidgeting. I wanted to check my watch but stopped myself, and that caused even more static for me.

Margot started sharing a story about her work with a family child care provider around working with families. I stepped in with both feet, offering my opinion and advice. I said that what she was planning on doing was not the right the thing to do.

She started taking notes furiously. I immediately knew that was wrong. We were going down the wrong path to building a partnership that I knew was critical to the success of our work together.

I took a breath, thought a moment, and then said: "Margot, I'm sorry I approached it this way with you. Can we start again? Will you tell me what you were thinking? I'm not in the field like you are. I don't see what you see. If I learn more from you about the situation, we can work together to reach our goal of supporting this teacher in her interactions with families."

Tychawn talks about the learning partnerships she creates with teachers. Video #9. Go to powerfulinteractions.com/coachingbook to access this video.

Principle Five: Modeling Matters— What You Say and Do Influences All Outcomes

We've chosen to put modeling as the last principle because, in your stance as coach, you model each of the other four principles as you approach your work. As a coach, what you decide to say and do matters, and, as noted earlier, it has a ripple effect that is felt by teachers and children.

Whether intentionally or not, when you work with teachers, what you say and do teaches them about teaching (Neuman & Cunningham 2009). Fred Rogers used to quote this Quaker saying: "Attitudes are caught, not taught." Every interaction you have with a teacher is an opportunity to show that teacher she is heard, respected, and appreciated, which is how we hope children feel too.

As you work with a teacher, you not only model behaviors, you model your stance, your beliefs or perspective about teaching and learning, and you encourage reflection. This may be even more important than any content you share. How you are with teachers will shape how they are with children. This is often described as a parallel process (Vella, Crowe, & Oades 2013).

When you recognize—and remember—the vital role that modeling plays in the lives of teachers and the children they interact with, you will become more effective as a coach.

Our colleagues in Arizona have adopted a key message to guide their work about modeling: *In Arizona's early childhood culture, we model Powerful Interactions with each other in ways that positively influence how all of us are with children.*

Modeling Supports Being Effective as a Coach

Learning happens within the context of relationships. When you engage with a teacher in the way you want him to engage in learning relationships with children, you strengthen your relationship with the teacher. You also enhance his ability to have similar interactions with children. This parallel process supports the teacher by providing clear examples he can focus on as he learns and changes in your work together.

✓ Reality Check

In Chapter 1 we discussed how as coach, you may have different roles or "wear different hats." Knowing how to be explicit about the hat you are wearing is essential to building a trusting relationship and a learning partnership.

Helena's story describes how a strengths-based perspective builds a good team. Video #10. Go to powerfulinteractions.com/coachingbook to access this video.

Modeling in Practice

Read the following stories about modeling. Notice how the coaches model the four principles we've discussed thus far, influencing outcomes for teachers and for children too.

A strengths-based coaching perspective searches for and highlights competence. In the video described on page 37, Helena tells a story about how believing that a teacher has strengths allows the teacher to recognize and share her own strengths.

Articulation gives teachers information they need to be more intentional. Sandy learned how modeling articulation allowed her to work with Karla to help 4-year-old Makini replace challenging behaviors with ones that were positive and acceptable:

> Karla teaches a class of 4-year-olds. She was struggling with Makini, whom she felt was exhibiting extremely challenging behavior. I was asked to visit to help her identify strategies that could help the child so that we might be able to transform a potential behavior problem into a learning opportunity.
>
> Once there, I began making notes and taking photos and videos of moments of effectiveness: the teachers' moments and the child's. At our debriefing, Karla, Leslie (the teacher assistant), and I formed a three-person team to collaborate and plan. The fact that I was modeling articulating practice in clear and accurate language gave us a way of approaching our work together.
>
> We reviewed the videos and focused our conversation on appreciating and noticing Makini's strengths and efforts. Together we articulated strategies to use more often so we could be more intentional about supporting him. Here are some of the strategies Karla and Leslie would try:
>
> - Focus on pausing in order to observe and plan their responses. We talked about the benefits of pausing versus reacting.
>
> - Minimize wait time, for example, during transitions. We talked about the benefits of peer modeling, play organizers, etc.
>
> - Give Makini more time to respond to directives in order to notice his attempts to "self-start." We talked about the benefits of allowing for processing time versus rushing him through the routines.

An Intentional Schedule

Sandy, a coach from Hawaii, shares this tip about learning partnerships.

"I now keep to a schedule so that teachers can be prepared for my visits. I used to drop in when it was good for me. Following an intentional schedule has created the opportunity for learning partnerships. And since teachers are prepared, I am noticing that they are taking the lead in the conversation. This is also new for me. When they take the lead, they talk more, ask more questions, and incorporate what we talk about into their lesson plans."

Coaching with Powerful Interactions

Three days later I went back. We began by sharing stories of Makini's successes. The teachers articulated more specific plans to allow Makini to make progress and to support his self-regulation and ability to self-start. These included plans to

- Support Makini's ability to attend by checking in with him using eye contact, public acknowledgment, and helping him pause as needed

- "Entice" his need to collect and transport objects by introducing a tube in the sensory tub

- Put a rope and pulley in the yard based on his recently expressed interest in the rope

We've got a lot of work ahead of us, but Makini and the team are moving ahead.

Articulation, the ability to be specific, lets us think as a team about how to move ahead. Our strategies are like markers on a path. We may change or adapt them but we know what they are.

Individualizing what you say and do allows you to build the respectful, trusting relationship needed for learning. Laura learned from a misstep that individualizing is vital to building positive relationships.

After conducting a formal classroom assessment with an experienced teacher, with whom I had a good relationship, I came to the debrief conversation with lots of notes and ideas about how the teacher could improve (there weren't many areas needing improvement). Afterwards, I sensed that the teacher seemed deflated, so I wrote her an email.

The teacher replied: "I wasn't going to say anything but since you brought it up, yes, I was upset." We agreed to talk.

After some small talk, I raised the issue. The teacher said that she didn't want to hurt my feelings. I replied that it isn't about my feelings. This is a professional conversation. I said I was open to feedback that would help me learn and grow as a coach.

Implicit and Explicit Modeling

As a coach you often use explicit modeling with a teacher. This means you and the teacher decide that you will "demonstrate" how to do a specific teaching practice such as using puppets to retell a story or preparing fruit salad with toddlers.

Implicit modeling, the focus of this chapter, is about being a certain way (what you say and do) with someone so that they can experience it and begin to integrate aspects of it into who they are and how they are with children. It's hard to teach someone to avoid being judgmental or defensive in conversations. But by being open-minded with that person and patient with their defensiveness, they may gradually be able to shift some aspects of their style and behaviors.

The teacher then said, "At our debrief, you just started talking. Had I known what our conversation was going to be about, I would have prepared. I would have brought examples of what I do so that we could talk from them."

My lessons learned for working with this thoughtful, skilled, and committed teacher include

- Plan ahead of time how and when we will debrief to give us both time to think and prepare

- Highlight strengths before jumping in

- Instead of telling the teacher how to address problem areas, say something like, "You show respect for children in many ways" and list them together. Then say, "Now let's think about ways you can let children know that you value their thinking."

When I apply these lessons, I can use the assessment to foster a two-way conversation.

Laura learned from this situation that she needed to ask the teacher how she would like to proceed with a discussion of the assessment results. Upon reflection, she also realized that she had decided that because she had a close relationship with the teacher, she could simply move ahead in an open way about changes—assuming the teacher would know that Laura respected her as a teacher. Where she misstepped was failing to realize that everyone needs to be seen and validated. Regardless of how well you know someone, you have to ask questions. The strategies Laura learned from this interaction are useful for all coaches working with any teacher.

A mutual learning partnership promotes shared responsibility and accountability. Monica shares this story:

> I make an intentional effort to model, describe, and talk about the three steps of a Powerful Interaction when coaching. This helps the teacher see our parallel process. Here is an example of what it looks like:

> I attend a meeting that caused static for me in the form of stress and worry. Then I rush to my next appointment—a coaching visit. I turn off the radio so I can have a moment to relax in the still silence of the car and focus on my breathing as I drive. This process allows me to let go of my static and get ready to be fully present with Julie, the teacher.

> As I enter Julie's classroom, I smile, greet her warmly, and comment on the changes I notice (new documentation panels that depict a project the children were working on). We take a seat, and I mention that in one of our prior conversations, she said she was working on quieting her static. I share with her my experience in the car. We both laugh and talk about how we are learning about and using the three steps of Powerful Interactions in our work.

In this chapter we have focused on **how** you are as a coach, which is determined in large part by your stance. In Chapter 3 we turn our attention to what you do in your work with a teacher to help the teacher enhance her practice and ultimately support the well-being and learning of young children.

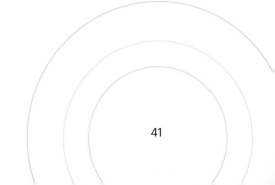

Chapter 3

Coaching with Powerful Interactions: The Three Steps

This chapter describes the three steps of coaching with Powerful Interactions: Be Present, Connect, and Extend Learning. It includes how your stance shapes the way you move through each step.

We encourage you to use the three steps whether you are corresponding with a teacher via email, having a brief conversation on the phone or in the hallway, doing a classroom observation, or having a feedback conversation. Keeping the steps in mind provides a roadmap for your interactions with teachers.

Lucy is an experienced teacher who is taking on a leadership role as she works on learning to effectively delegate responsibilities to her student teachers and others who support children with special needs in her classroom of toddlers. Let's take a look as Michael, her supervisor and coach, uses the three steps of Powerful Interactions to guide their work together. You'll see how he uses the three steps in her classroom and in their feedback conversation later that afternoon. Notice how he uses coaching to support her goal of delegating and is able to do so because of the many adults in the classroom.

The first step of coaching with Powerful Interactions is to Be Present. Quieting your static lets you hold onto your coaching stance, pause, and make decisions about how to Connect.

Michael coaches Lucy using the three steps of Powerful Interactions. Video #11. Go to powerfulinteractions.com/coachingbook to access this video, the other videos in this book, and bonus material.

Step One: Be Present to Coach

Though this step may sound simple, many people tell us, "Being present is a big challenge!" In today's busy world, many people may find this difficult. It takes a conscious decision and effort to focus and lots of practice to be present at least some of the time, beginning with quieting the static.

Static interferes with the ability to Be Present. It leads to reacting. It can often lead to dashing here and there to "put out fires," in contrast to being present and responding in a purposeful or intentional way.

Static affects us all. It's everywhere—at home, at work, and places in between! It is prevalent in all aspects of our lives. It grows louder whenever too many people and too many things demand your attention—now! When static gets loud it can undermine your desire to connect. Doing so feels too difficult, even painful. Your energy has to go to cutting through the static. This leaves little room for connecting and building the relationship that is so vital to working together effectively. This is true for you and for the teacher you are coaching.

For example, Kendra, the director of a large child care program, always begins a meeting or one-on-one interaction by talking about what is going on with her. When asked about it, Kendra said it was her way of personalizing her interactions, of building relationships. But when observed, it became clear everything she said was about her. She needed this time to shift gears, cut through the static, and be able to focus on the people and issues at hand. The problem was that instead of personalizing, Kendra's behavior was causing frustration and resentment among staff; they wanted to connect and felt their time was being wasted.

✓ Reality Check

Many coaches have shared that there are times when it is almost impossible to quiet the static. If you coach in a large program or school district, maintaining a schedule can often be impossible. Unexpected meetings or other interruptions to your planned schedule are practically a given. In many instances this may mean that you can't keep appointments with teachers. Rather than feeling overwhelmed, angry, and guilty that you are shirking your primary responsibility to teachers, it can be helpful to let go and roll with the situation. Write a friendly email to the teacher letting her know that circumstances beyond your control have prevented you from visiting. Invite her to send you a picture of something she's been working on and try to have an email correspondence to keep the momentum of your conversation going. Other coaches have described how personal life situations can be such that the static is overwhelming. Sometimes talking with colleagues to vent and then deciding how to move forward can calm the static.

Reflections

Being aware of static is the first step toward reducing it!

Think about what causes static for you.

Think about what causes static for the person you are coaching.

Now reflect on those you coach. In what ways would they say you are trustworthy?

Quieting the inner noise of static is the key to Michael's effectiveness as a coach. Video #12. Go to powerfulinteractions.com/coachingbook to access this video.

If you decide that the quality of your relationships is important because the relationships will advance your work with teachers, then you have to find a way to turn the static into background music. This is necessary so you can focus on the person or people in front of you. A focused interaction that lasts a few minutes has endless positive possibilities.

Do a Quick Me Check

To be present and prepare for a Powerful Interaction, do a quick Me Check. Ask yourself two questions:

- How am I feeling now?
- How can I adjust to fit and connect with the other person?

Once you get the hang of it, a Me Check takes less than a minute.

Let's take a closer look at each of the Me Check questions.

How am I feeling now? By first focusing on yourself, on the inside, you're able to make more deliberate decisions and to respond rather than react.

How you answer this question probably changes throughout the day. Think about all the things that can affect your mood. Some factors might be

- The ups and downs of your work day: You just had a coaching session that you thought would be challenging, and it went really well. You haven't completed some forms your supervisor needs by the end of the day. You have a conference at noon with a teacher who's often late. You have multiple projects at work that need attention now, but you are wondering how you will get to the grocery store before it's time to pick up your daughter at school.
- What's going on in your life outside of work: You're packing up your house because you're moving on Saturday. You and your spouse had an argument last night. You're planning an exciting vacation.
- Your health and well-being: You've got this cough that's been lingering for weeks. Your back hurts like crazy, and it's really hard to sit on a small chair when you observe in a classroom. You're antsy because you haven't exercised for days.

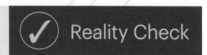

Reality Check

When you have a planned meeting with a teacher, it is easier to be conscious of clearing the static. Sometimes a teacher just stops by or meets you in the hallway and begins discussing a concern—an unexpected interaction. It can be really hard to clear the static or even remember to do so. In situations like this, it is sometimes best to respond to the teacher by saying, "I really want to hear the issue you are sharing with me. Can we make a time later today to discuss it? Then I know I can give you my full attention."

Coaching with Powerful Interactions

After looking inside and thinking about how you are feeling, the second Me Check question involves looking outside yourself and thinking about how you'll create a comfortable fit with the other person.

How can I adjust to fit and connect with the other person? You adjust yourself to fit with family members and friends all the time, often without knowing you're doing so. When your spouse arrives home at the end of the day and you sense he is upset, you may quiet your excitement from your day so you can greet him a little more calmly than you were envisioning. When one of your children runs over to show you the beautiful rock she found on the beach, you put aside thoughts of what you are going to make for dinner. Instead, you smile, and your eyes light up to share her pleasure.

As a Powerful Interactions coach, a principle that underlies your coaching stance is individualizing. Part of your role is to intentionally adjust to create a "just right fit" with the teacher you are coaching. You might adjust

- Your tone of voice
- The pace of the interaction
- Your energy level
- How many words you use
- The length of pauses between exchanges
- The expressions on your face

Many times it will be easy and feel natural. But there will be times, especially with people whose behaviors can push your buttons, you may find that it takes extra effort to find the best fit possible.

Whether adjustments are easy or challenging, they make positive connections possible. And positive connections pave the way for Powerful Interactions. Powerful Interactions cannot unfold without positive connections.

It is impossible to create a "just right fit" all the time. You may be tired, frustrated with a colleague, or upset about something going on at home. Doing a Me Check gives you a moment to put aside your own issues.

Reality Check

Many coaches have described how difficult it can be to work with a teacher whose philosophy about teaching differs from their own. When this is the case, avoid making it a personal issue. Your role as coach is to highlight the impact of the teacher's actions on children's learning. If, for example, a toddler teacher calls for cleanup with no notice, interrupting toddlers' play, and leading to frustration and challenging behaviors, you might want to videotape a child's reaction to being interrupted. Then find a quiet time to view and discuss it together. You can also refer to research about the value of smooth transitions and positive guidance to emphasize the importance of giving toddlers sufficient warning so that they have a sense of control, an important part of learning self-regulation.

Step Two: Connecting as a Coach

Moments of connection are the building blocks of relationships. When people feel connected, they feel seen, heard, recognized, and acknowledged. Paying careful attention to your first conversation with a teacher lays the foundation for the trust that you will build with her over time. This trust is vital to the success of your work together.

As your coaching relationship gets underway, everyday moments—a greeting in the morning, a question about how things are going, a smile or nod, an email—can be easy to overlook, yet each is an opportunity to connect. Moments of connection can take many other forms as well. For example, you might take a photo of a teacher and send it in a text message or share a smile as you both watch a child accomplish a challenging task.

At a staff meeting at Wintonbury Early Childhood Magnet School in Connecticut, teachers told us about what might help them connect with a coach and build trust during a classroom visit. Here's what they had to say about connecting:

> Let me know ahead of time when you want to visit. That way I have time to think and prepare.
>
> When entering my classroom, please do the following:
>
> - Try to Be Present. I will try to Be Present too. Clearing static is a two-way street.
>
> - Wait a moment and I will introduce you to the children when the time is right. Avoid grand entrances. They can distract everyone.
>
> - Be aware it makes me nervous to be observed.
>
> - Take note of the time you are visiting and how that might impact what you see. For example, is it the day after a weeklong break? During a transition between activities?
>
> - Remember that I am focused on my interactions with children. I will interact with you when I can. When I do, recognize that I need to shift from talking with children to talking with an adult.
>
> - Ask yourself, "Should I stay or go?" or "Should I engage with the teacher at this time or leave a note with strengths-based comments about my observations and/or questions?"

- Decide with me about where in the classroom you can leave a written communication.

It is a good idea to talk with the teachers you are coaching about additional ideas that you both can use to connect. It is a conversation that in itself creates a connection. Over time, moments of connection add up to strong, positive relationships that are a prerequisite for effective coaching.

Monica Brinkerhoff highlights the importance of connecting with teachers and relates it to the principle of learning partnerships:

> Connecting with teachers is a critical step in the process of change. Connecting requires emotional intelligence. As a coach, I must be able to read what a teacher might be feeling, be aware of and set aside my own assumptions and beliefs to support growth, and help build on the teacher's motivation. For me, it is critical that I recognize and celebrate the capacity of teachers. I approach the coaching relationship expecting to learn as much from the people I'm coaching as they learn from me, and I take the time to communicate that. I begin our work together by explaining my mental model of coaching, including my stance of co-learning. I let them know that their goals for learning are what will drive our work together. As Margaret Wheatley notes, people change when the change is meaningful and important to them (Wheatley 2001).

On the pages that follow, you'll learn about three strategies to use to connect with teachers. The following strategies and connections can help you to build positive relationships that will provide the security a teacher needs to be open to exploring, experimenting, discovering, and learning in your work together:

1. Be Trustworthy

2. Listen to Learn

3. Communicate to Form Partnerships

We describe each strategy separately so you can think about each one. In reality, you'll likely use them with one another. For example, when you are trustworthy, it is very likely that you listen to learn and communicate in a way that promotes a partnership between you and the teacher.

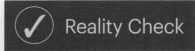
Reality Check

You may not like every teacher. You may disagree with a teacher's philosophy or some of her practices. You don't have to be best friends. But you are responsible for building a positive connection with each teacher (just as teachers are expected to do with every child).

Connect Strategy One: Be Trustworthy

If we want others to trust us, the first step is to be trustworthy. The second step is to show that we are trustworthy: we have to provide enough intelligible evidence of competence, honesty, and reliability in the relevant matters for others to reach an intelligent judgment. (O'Neill 2013)

Relationships grow with trust. We trust someone we can rely on—someone who is steady and dependable. Trustworthy individuals follow through, keep their word, and are there when we need them. As O'Neill notes, the person you coach needs consistent evidence of your trustworthiness in order to be open to learning from and with you.

Louis Mark Romei, a colleague who coaches teachers working with preschoolers who are dual language learners, shares these insights about being trustworthy in the coaching relationship:

I believe that if the teacher feels that her coach is a partner with her, trust has been established. In my personal interactions with the teachers I support as a coach, I always share my past experiences, funny stories, and anecdotes of things that worked or didn't work. I think this helps them see that although I don't have my own classroom anymore, I still "get it." I'm on their side. I've been there. I'm there with them now, and together we'll move forward. Something as simple as giving teachers my cell phone number has also helped. I haven't shared it with all teachers, but some send me a quick text with a question. Little things like this help to build and maintain trust. We're there for each other, and the teacher truly knows it.

Another aspect of trust between a coach and teacher is when the teacher feels that she is a priority. This means when a date for a meeting or classroom visit is set, both parties have checked their schedules to see if it works and both parties do their best to keep the meeting or visit. If it can't work, it's rescheduled for a later day or time. Your actions need to model that the work is important. When coaches cancel visits or meetings at the last minute or without letting the teacher know, this communicates something to teachers, and it's not good.

Tychawn offers her insights into what it means to be trustworthy. Video #13. Go to powerfulinteractions.com/coachingbook to access this video.

Trust builds when you are sincere about wanting to highlight a teacher's strengths and when you are genuine in your desire to nurture the learning partnership.

Trust is a two-way street. While you take the lead, ultimately the relationship grows when you are both willing to engage with each other. Monica Charlie, a coaching colleague from Arizona, offers this important insight as well: "Trust is built upon the willingness of both people to risk being open in their interactions with each other."

Trusting relationships are built upon shared understandings. You and the teacher might think of these as ground rules or mutually acceptable terms for your work together. In other words, they are the decisions you jointly make about how you will work together. This is reciprocity, which might include jointly establishing a plan that addresses the frequency and pattern of your sessions. You might decide together that you will visit the teacher every two weeks, spend a half hour observing in her classroom, and then meet at nap time for a feedback conversation.

In trusting relationships, coaches are transparent about their role and the work they will do with teachers. To be transparent means to begin a conversation about the purpose of the work you and the teacher will do together. This is a critical time to highlight your shared purpose. You are in a learning partnership on behalf of the success of all children and their families. During this conversation it is vital to agree on the expectations for how you will work together. This should begin with a discussion of goal setting and the need for the teacher to feel ownership of the goals. Talk about how often you'll meet, when you'll observe, and that you'll have feedback sessions. You can use your coaching conversations as opportunities for both coach and teacher to think and talk about your feelings about your relationship and how your work is going. We will talk more about setting goals and expectations for working together in "Step Three: Coaching to Extend Learning," in the section called "Extend Learning Strategy One: Focus on Goals You Set Together."

Your stance can help: "High trust connections can inspire greatness. Such connections free up teachers to take on new challenges by virtue of the safety net they create" (Tschannen-Moran & Tschannen-Moran 2011a, 13).

> ## Your Coaching Stance: Be Trustworthy
>
> You demonstrate that you're trustworthy when you
>
> • Use a teacher's strengths as the foundation of your conversations and work together
>
> • Individualize your interactions to address a teacher's personal style, experience, language, culture, needs, and interests
>
> • Acknowledge that you too are a learner in the partnership

Transparency

What coaches have to say about transparency

Sandy: Trust is built by letting the other person know there is no hidden agenda.

Angela: The ability to be transparent is key in a trusting relationship. However, this requires a certain degree of vulnerability on the part of the person who is being transparent. While it's easy to be transparent when you are sharing positive feedback, it is much more difficult when the feedback or the circumstance (or sometimes your role) requires you to deliver "more constructive" feedback. In these situations, if trust has not been established, it is hard to have an honest conversation about the work. To be most effective, trust, and transparency, should be reciprocal.

Shannon: I recently made attempts to approach the relationships with a level of transparency and found that this conflicted with some coachees' assumptions. They questioned and challenged my intentions. I found this disheartening. Why do we so often assume ulterior motives of one another? What is it that we are experiencing in life that leads us to this view?

Be trustworthy: Stories from the field. Sandy tells about how her static interfered with her ability to convey trustworthiness. Once she quieted her static, she could build trust:

I was asked to return to a preschool classroom to help teachers objectively observe and be able to support a child who thinks and learns differently. Although the teachers and I had worked well together the week before, I spent the weekend getting ready for this second visit.

When I walked in the room, I felt that the teachers were not open to coaching. It was icy! Bbrrrrr. On this second visit, they didn't really want to talk.

My first inclination went to "Oh my." I tried to let go of my static. I stepped out of the room to text Judy, who was mentoring me as a coach. She wasn't there, but in the seconds it took to send the text, I caught my breath. And I began to remember—my work was about the teacher and the keiki (children). Not about me. Or my agenda. Or even the weekend I'd spent preparing for this visit.

Once I did that, my static was quiet. I stepped back in, smiled and could feel that the teachers and I connected. (Tschannen-Moran & Tschannen-Moran 2011a, 13).

Later that day as we talked at nap time, one teacher said, "We didn't trust you. We thought the "I notice" statements from last week were a ploy . . . and you were going to criticize us today because there is an issue to think about."

They asked me to come back again the following week to discuss what I had originally planned for that day.

It takes time to build trust and relationships.

Tips for being trustworthy. Realistically, it takes more than following a few tips for someone to come to see you as trustworthy. Nonetheless, keeping these suggestions in mind can be helpful, especially in the midst of all you do in your coaching role:

- Do what you say you'll do. Trust grows when you're dependable and when the relationship has rhythm and predictability. Suggestions from coaches include

  - Follow through in a timely way. For example, if you offer resources to a teacher, let her know when you will deliver them and be sure to do so.

  - Recognize that what builds trust isn't how much time you spend with a teacher, but rather how reliable and steady you are.

  - Create a schedule for visits and stick with it. Karen shares: "I used to just show up when it was convenient for my schedule. I realize now that I need a schedule and have to stick to it. Teachers want to know when to expect me. If we have a date, I have to show up. If a situation comes up that interferes with the schedule, I text or call with a message of apology and reschedule."

- Be genuine and show appreciation for work teachers do. Always leave a little note or send a text or email describing something you notice in the teacher's setting. It is a way of conveying: "I see you and the effort you are making on behalf of children and families." You might text a quick message: "Saw photos you posted in the art area to extend children's explorations of clay; children referred to them with excitement as they created clay figures."

- Help without judgment. If you decide that lending another pair of hands will move the relationship and trust forward, offer it in neutral and straightforward manner. You might ask, "Jocelyn, would it be helpful if I took photos of the babies enjoying their walk in the neighborhood so we can post them where their families can see what their children did today?"

Reflections

Think of a person in your life whom you feel is trustworthy. What is it about that person that makes you think so?

What does that person do and say to demonstrate trust?

Now reflect on those you coach. In what ways would they say you are trustworthy?

Sometimes it is difficult to connect with a teacher. Building a trusting relationship takes time and patience—it doesn't happen after one visit. Remember, it is your job to go slowly and be patient with the intention to make the relationship work.

Sometimes a teacher may not want to be coached or is afraid of being found lacking in skills. Perhaps she had a negative experience with another coach and "knows how bad coaching can be." When you can resist taking the teacher's responses personally, and simply be present and open, you can use the tips offered here to gradually strengthen a relationship.

- Recognize boundaries. Often coaching conversations start off with the teacher sharing a personal problem. There are times when that is as far as the conversation gets. Angela Zilch from Arizona said, "Sometimes the coaching interaction becomes enmeshed by the personal relationship." Listening to the teacher to demonstrate that she is heard can help her quiet her static. Just remember that the connection you have is based on shared work together—extending the teacher's learning on behalf of children. Be sure to notice when it is time to move on to the agenda that the two of you had set for the conversation. Sometimes a coach shares a personal challenge as a way to show her own vulnerability. Be sure to highlight the example and how it relates to the teacher's situation and then move back to talking about the teacher and her work.

- Recognize that we all make judgments and use yours to help you see the positive. It's human nature to make judgments. As you enter a classroom, listen to your first impression. Then imagine what you would want to see. Look for that and chances are you will find an example, even a small one, of what you hope for.

This is especially important with teachers who challenge you. For example, if your first impression is that

- The room is cluttered and there seems to be no organization, focus on looking for one example of organization, such as a plastic container holding the markers or a rug where the kindergartners sit for group time and reading

- The displays are mostly commercial and nothing is displayed at children's eye level, focus on looking for one piece of children's art or writing hanging on the wall where children can easily see it

- The teacher has an almost angry look on her face and she never seems to be at infants' eye level, focus on looking for a moment in which she smiles, perhaps at another staff person or even at you

- Own your mistakes. There is nothing like finger pointing or assigning fault to undermine trust. Did you arrive late to a visit? Miss a visit? Forget that book on early math teaching strategies that you promised? If you make a mistake, acknowledge it in a matter-of-fact way. If a teacher makes a mistake, encourage her to do the same.

Connect Strategy Two: Listen to Learn

How do you feel when someone really listens to you? Isn't it wonderful when someone not only is listening to you, but also really understands what you're saying and feeling, too?

Being listened to and feeling understood is a basic human need—the foundation of safe and trusting relationships. And feeling like we haven't been listened to or are being ignored and misunderstood is painful whether we are 5 or 50.

Yet research shows that "many listeners rely too much on short-term memory during the listening process. Researchers in the field of communication have found that individuals recall only 50 percent of a message immediately after listening to it and only 25 percent after a short delay" (Pearson et al. 2011, 113).

Often people say that someone trustworthy is someone who really listens. Listening is more than just hearing. It means deciding to pay attention and to find meaning in what someone says—or doesn't say—with her words or body language. Listening requires a genuine exchange of give-and-take. Active listening takes focus and energy. You have to put aside your agenda and assumptions so that you can be open to what the other person is trying to tell you.

Listen to learn: Stories from the field. In this story, Clarissa realized that she wasn't listening. This awareness allowed her to listen, connect, and learn.

> I realize now that when I enter a teacher's classroom, I'm often not in an open, quiet listening-and-observing-to-learn mode. I tend to form quick impressions and jump right into things. Today I made a conscious effort to stand back and watch. It was amazing—I actually was able to pay attention to how Megan and her assistant, Talia, work together.
>
> Pausing allowed me to catch my breath and to shift my thoughts to focus on Megan and the children. I was able to listen more so that I could take better notes. I could see that Megan, too, was working on listening to children.
>
> After the visit, I emailed Megan. I asked her to identify examples of times she paused and moments when she was really connecting with the children so that we could talk about connecting at our next visit.

Your Coaching Stance: Listen to Learn

You are more likely to listen to learn when you

- Are open to hearing strengths
- Quiet the temptation to form judgments
- Focus on the specific actions the teacher describes so that you can help her articulate her intentionality
- Individualize how you listen and respond to fit a teacher's personal style and temperament (for example, some teachers may need longer periods of quiet than others to pull their thoughts together. Others may appreciate prompt questions to draw them out. One size doesn't fit all.)
- Trust that you can learn from the teacher and let the teacher know when you are learning

I realized my pause let me connect and learn more about Megan. This knowledge will help us look more closely at her interactions with children.

Diana tells the following story about how she put her judgments and assumptions aside—after some effort on her part—and learned something new about a teacher.

I remember a professional development exercise on listening. We worked in pairs: one partner was the talker, the other the listener. Then we were to switch.

I partnered with a woman who is known for talking a lot. My role was listener for the first round. I wasn't supposed to say anything but could indicate my interest and that I was listening. Of course she didn't need any prompting.

As I listened she pretty much answered all the questions I would have asked. It was very interesting. Because she is always talking, I realized I don't always listen to her. But she taught me something this day: If I sit and listen, people can say things I want to know. I now try harder to close my mouth and listen—and to focus on what a teacher is saying, instead of my questions. I'm not always successful but I try more to listen.

Tips for listening to learn. When you really listen to teachers and stay open in order to learn, you can see and appreciate them in a way that you can't when you assume you know them and what they are going to say. Here are some tips to help you be a more effective and open listener:

- Convey the message, "I hear you." Making sounds like "uh-huh" and "um-hmm" from time to time lets the speaker know you are following the meaning. A nod, raised eyebrows, and a smile communicate that the speaker has your attention. Sometimes a single word like "Really" or "Interesting" can encourage the speaker to continue.

- Keep an open mind. Set assumptions and judgments aside. Express your curiosity. If you hear something you disagree with or even are offended, it can be hard to continue listening and avoid becoming defensive. Try to stay calm and Be Present so you can continue to hear what the teacher is saying and try to understand the intent behind his words and gestures.

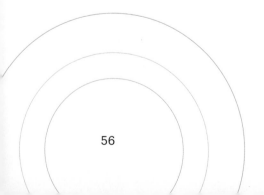

- Ask for additional information. Simple phrases like "Tell me more" or "And then what happened?" spark the speaker to elaborate on her thinking. Avoid questions that challenge what the speaker has said so that she doesn't become defensive. For example, "How could you have thought that?" is likely to make someone feel criticized.

- Think about how you look when listening. Your face and body language convey that you are interested in what someone is telling you. To do this, maintain a relaxed and open facial expression. Sometimes people who think they look interested can unintentionally look annoyed. Sometimes in your eagerness to attend, you lean forward, but you might be intruding on the speaker's personal space.

- Take notes while listening. Writing notes lets the speaker know that you're taking your role as listener seriously. You can use your notes to offer the person an instant replay of their ideas. After the teacher finishes a thought, articulate by referring to your notes. You might say to a kindergarten teacher, "You just described an effective teaching strategy. You respond to children's interests by reading their journals, noting topics they write about, and then choosing stories to read aloud that build on their interests."

- Be open to ways that culture may affect listening. Like many things, how you listen to others is influenced by culture. To understand diversity we need to be aware of our own prejudices and assumptions. Sometimes it's hard to talk about things that make us uncomfortable, and unfortunately, culture is often one of those things. Things we don't know about can also make us uncomfortable. In some cultures, people talk directly to each other, expressing themselves verbally. In others, people communicate indirectly, conveying messages through a third party, or through symbols, metaphors, or silence. Listening is the basic form of respect for others. Through listening, we put ourselves aside for a moment and try to understand and, if possible, empathize with another person. Active listening is both an art and a critical skill. Remember, how you are as an open listener models how the teacher can be with children and families. In the video described on this page, Helena shares an insight about culture.

- Check for understanding. Paraphrasing—or using different words to summarize—is one way to see if you understand the meaning of what a person says. You might say, "So what I hear you saying is . . ." You can also seek clarity by saying, "Please tell me more about what you mean. I'm not sure I understand."

Reflections

How Well Do I Really Listen?

Can I quiet my mind and my voice long enough to really listen to someone else?

Do I get restless when I get bored listening or when there's silence?

Do I tend to interrupt the speaker?

When is listening hard to do?

How do I know when I am truly listening? What do I do? How do I feel?

Helena describes how she works with teachers to support their learning about culture. Video #14. Go to powerfulinteractions.com/coachingbook to access this video.

Or perhaps try, "I want to understand exactly what you mean. Can you say it another way?" Or you could ask for an example, "What might this look like in your classroom?"

- Minimize distractions. Often conversations between coaches and teachers take place in the classroom during nap time. To model the importance of quieting the static so that the conversation between you is central, you could start the conversation with, "I realize that you are in the middle of an incredibly busy day. Shall we take a minute so that you can focus on our conversation?" Or you might suggest, "Let's put our phones away or on vibrate so that we can focus on our conversation."

- Allow pauses for thinking. Sometimes a teacher pauses to gather her thoughts and the coach who is listening either asks a question too soon or changes the subject. Resist interrupting, as this models the importance of being patient when listening.

- Quiet your own agenda. In the words of one coach, "I know I struggle with my agenda. When I'm listening, sometimes I am thinking, 'Okay, let's get through this and get to what's really important.'" If your own thoughts keep distracting you, try to let them go. Take a deep breath. Pick up your pen and write down each comment that the teacher makes to help you focus on her. Another coach said, "I have a tendency to personalize what someone is telling me. I catch myself often thinking, 'Oh, I want to tell how I handled that' or 'Oh, the same thing happened to me.' I find that if I can stop myself from blurting that out, I can remain focused on the person I'm listening to."

Jill describes how quieting her agenda helps create a Powerful Interactions climate. Video #15. Go to powerfulinteractions.com/coachingbook to access this video.

Connect Strategy Three: Communicate to Form Partnerships

Can you recall a time when you tried to convey a message to someone but what the person heard wasn't what you intended? Or you might recall the opposite situation. Perhaps you were hurt or offended by someone's message, but it turned out that what you understood wasn't the other person's intended message.

Everything about how you communicate conveys your stance as a coach and builds or deepens your relationships with others. Communication is a complex process that involves different components:

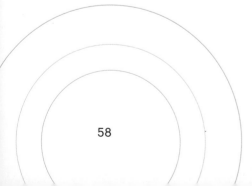

Coaching with Powerful Interactions

- Word choice
- Tone
- Inflection
- Pace
- Delivery
- Loud or soft voice

We communicate nonverbally as well as verbally. Nonverbal communication includes our body language, facial expressions, gestures, and silences. Often we are unaware of the messages we send through nonverbal communication, and what we intend to convey is not what the person perceives.

Culture is another factor that affects communication. Our culture includes our beliefs about ourselves, and our attitudes, assumptions, and expectations about people and events around us. It influences how and what we see, what interests us, what annoys us or frustrates us as we communicate with other people. Each of us sees and hears through our own unique eyes, ears, and mind. When you understand your culture and how it affects you as a communicator, you are more likely to ask questions than make assumptions. Your communication is more likely to be individualized to the person with whom you are speaking, which can lead to a more trusting relationship and a stronger learning partnership.

Lucy, a toddler teacher, offers this inspiring insight about culture: "Whenever the opportunity presents itself, we should always take advantage of learning from different cultures. Diversity enriches all relationships and organizations by bringing together different ideas and life experiences."

Try to use the same tone and style for all feedback to strengthen the learning partnership and lead to conversations. This limits the "teachy and preachy" and defensiveness. For example,

To highlight strengths, you might say, "I notice that when it was time to go to the media center, you immediately got the kindergartners engaged in a rhyming song. I could see how quickly it got their attention and helps them learn phonemic awareness."

Reality Check

Sometimes it is hard to listen to someone. You might find the person boring or very long-winded. Focus on noticing the person's strengths. Listen for the nugget. Pay attention to clues that you have stopped listening. They may include having thoughts such as

- I am feeling irritated.
- I want to get this person out of the way.
- I am too busy for this.
- Hurry up. I have more important things to do.
- What am I going to make for dinner?

Your Coaching Stance: Communication

Effective communication is two-way and critical to a strengths-based approach. You are more likely to communicate to form a partnership by

• Starting a conversation with an "I notice" statement to validate the teacher's strengths

• Calling attention to intentionality by using facts to describe the teacher's actions and the impact they have on children's learning

• Posing a question that invites the teacher to talk about her decision-making

• Checking in with the teacher about how she would be most comfortable communicating: face-to-face, in emails or texts, or by phone

To invite a teacher to reflect on what she says and does, you might say, "I heard you saying to children, 'You are so smart.' Let's think. What did you notice about their specific actions?" You might go on to say, "I'm interested in the decisions you made that led to Yancey's trying out new materials for the obstacle course. If we can articulate together some of the decisions you made that resulted in his willingness to try something new, you'll be able to use those strategies with greater intention in the future."

When you have a concern about a teacher's words or actions, you might say, "I noticed that you asked Joey and Caleb to be partners. I'm interested in learning about that decision." Then listen and follow up by saying, "I wonder what else you could have done to help both children succeed. What do you think?"

Communicate to form a partnership: Stories from the field. Diana shares the following story about how communicating helped her form a partnership and friendship with a colleague, much to her surprise, and ended up influencing her work as a coach.

When you quiet the static, you can be present to create a common ground or find a bridge between yourself and another person. Fifteen years ago, I met a colleague. She's as different from me as you could imagine. She has a quirky haircut and was a rock star groupie at the time. Her clothes are bright with a dramatic flair. Mine are shades of taupe and black.

We were working in a small group and I thought, "Who is this person?" She doesn't look like any of my friends. I listened, and divine intervention led me to look beyond her appearance to learn about who she is and her practice.

She's a friend and colleague today. She's brilliant. She makes life a party, and I need that sometimes. If I had based my decisions on what I saw with my eyes, I would have missed getting to know her and our relationship.

This experience has carried over as I work with teachers. I realize it is easy to take on attitudes and prejudices even without being aware of doing so or thinking of yourself as the kind of person who does. And yet there is so much wisdom and knowledge you can learn from others. Sometimes when a teacher is talking and I'm about to roll my eyes—at least inwardly—I pause, listen harder, and find there is something to learn, and our partnership grows.

Tips to communicate to form a partnership. Deciding to be more intentional about how you communicate is a first step in improving your communication skills. Here are some tips that can support you in your efforts to demonstrate respect, recognize the expertise of others, and ensure that you have two-way conversations.

- Provide a predictable structure for conversations. Whether you are writing an email or talking face-to-face, think about the three steps of a Powerful Interaction.

- Pay close attention to the words you use. *Brainstorm, collaborate, co-create,* or *think together* all communicate that you know you have as much to learn from the coaching relationship as the person you are coaching.

- Keep the conversation going. Follow up on previous conversations and revisit the goals discussed. Check in about issues that have been discussed.

- Pause between comments. This conveys the importance of think time and supports two-way conversations.

- Write notes about what you want to say. One coach said, "If I don't write down the feedback I want to offer and my questions, I tend to ramble. It takes me way too many words to get an idea across. When I write down my 'I notice' statements in advance, I remember to be succinct and I don't go on and on saying the same thing 30 different ways."

- Keep your emotions in check. Be sure to mentally prepare for a challenging conversation. If something comes up in the moment and taps into your emotions, it is easy to be abrupt. In the heat of the moment, a good technique is to say, "I can hear that this is an important topic, and I want to really listen and think with you about it. Let's talk about it [in an hour or at the end of the day]. That way we can both think about it some more and put our heads together to find a solution." When you are alone, think about the issue from the other person's perspective. Look for the strength in what the person is saying. Begin the conversation by paraphrasing what you heard (without emotion), and then say, "Let's think about this together."

- Be sure there is understanding. As with listening, communication is a two-way street. Pause often as you convey a message; this allows the other person to respond and gives you a chance to check to make sure your conversation partner is with you.

Tychawn and Helena talk about communicating effectively. Video #16. Go to powerfulinteractions.com/coachingbook to access this video.

Reflections

Invite a trusted colleague to videotape you having a conversation with a teacher. View it with your colleague. How do you look? How do you sound? Are there any intentional shifts you want to make to be a more effective communicator? If you are willing to take the risk, view it with the teacher and talk about how to strengthen your partnership through communication.

Sometimes we're caught off guard and we blow it. When this happens, apologize.

Karen shares this insight: "Recently I was thinking that we all have a choice to be reactive or responsive. If we choose to be reactive, that may deal with the person's situation at that moment in time but won't necessarily empower him to handle the next situation. And if we are responsive, we may not solve his problem for him, but he will walk away empowered, supported, and heard."

- Avoid labels, jargon, and shorthand. If you want someone to understand what you mean, use straightforward, factual language. If, for example, we say that "articulation leads to intentionality," we have to be able to model language that communicates that message so it is understandable to all.

- Fit the teacher's style. Think about where you will meet. If the teacher is easily distracted, it is important to find a quiet location. Be flexible if the teacher feels more comfortable staying in his classroom while children are napping. Remember that the coaching conversation is about you and the teacher communicating in a way that makes it easier and more accessible for him. A neutral location is often a good idea. For example, you might meet in an office that isn't being used, in the cafeteria, or outside if weather permits.

Manage Your Time

When it comes to communication, longer isn't better. Steadiness and predictability build relationships and keep the conversation going.

Step Three: Coaching to Extend Learning

No matter **what** you want to teach, **how** you interact influences the teacher's receptivity to learning from what you model or discuss.

Imagine that you meet a teacher for a brief, spontaneous hallway conversation or a planned coaching session. You've intentionally quieted your static and made a connection. As you deepen your relationship with this teacher, you transform an interaction into a Powerful Interaction by extending the teacher's learning.

Grounded in a strengths-based perspective, you quickly reflect on the teacher's strengths. By putting them into words—articulating the strengths—you offer information you believe will help her to be more intentional and effective. You think about who she is and how you can individualize to build trust and support her learning. Then as her learning partner, you offer feedback, information, or a question—in a way that is just right for her—that can lead the teacher to stretch her thinking and learning.

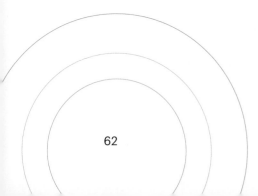

Coaching with Powerful Interactions

This step—coaching to extend learning—is a two-way professional development conversation. It is within this context that you apply four interrelated Extend Learning strategies to stretch teachers' learning:

1. Focus on goals you set together.

2. Notice moments of effectiveness.

3. Use prompts and questions to encourage thinking together.

4. Document plans and progress together.

A Powerful Interactions coaching relationship is a learning conversation over time that focuses on reflecting, exploring, analyzing, and digging deeper into good practice. This is a notable shift from thinking about "training" as how we extend the learning of adults.

The Extend Learning step is an opportunity to change reflections into insights, expand knowledge into wisdom, and inspire changes in behavior that improve performance. Michelangelo once noted that there is a statue inside every block of marble, and it was his challenge to find it. Similarly, it is the coach's role to find the effective educator and leader inside every teacher.

It's easy for coaches to get caught up with the frustrations of coaching and spend time venting with each other. However, staying in the "vent" space restricts the possibilities for your own learning and having energy to extend a teacher's learning.

Tara, Michael, and Diana describe their venting and how they manage it to move their work ahead. Video #17. Go to powerfulinteractions.com/coachingbook to access this video.

Demystifying "Extend Learning"

Many coaches and teachers alike express concern that the Extend Learning step of a Powerful Interaction has to be significant. As our friend and colleague Charlotte Stetson says, "Extend Learning simply means stretching someone's learning just a little bit." For teachers, you don't have to "teach" them something new and exciting that they can add to their repertoire. It can be small and simple, yet meaningful!

• You invite the teacher to pay attention to a decision she made and you offer language to describe it: "When you held and rocked her gently, you let her know that she can depend on you to keep her safe."

• You help her see that she engaged children in mathematical thinking as she played a transition game to get them lined up for outside time.

• Because the teacher is interested in exploring what children learn through dramatic play, you suggest that she spend time observing children at play to consider new props she might add to extend their involvement and learning.

Sometimes your own static gets in the way of extending a teacher's learning. Here are a few examples of what coaches have said:

• "I was drowning in a backlog of paperwork and had to make the classroom observation anyway. I just couldn't focus on the visit and wished I'd postponed it so that I could finish the paperwork first."

• "I was upset that my daughter was going to school not feeling well and kept watching my cell phone during my feedback session with the teacher. I heard nothing she said. In retrospect, I wish I'd told her what was up, then said, 'Hey, I'd like to keep my phone on the table in case the school calls.' Then I'd have conveyed to her that I'm human, too, and modeled how to move on to work at hand."

• "I walked into the center and noticed a supervision issue. A toddler was climbing on the back of the couch and no one was nearby. I went over, gave him my hand, and led him to the block area. When I let the teachers know what I had observed, my annoyance and blame came across in my tone. In retrospect, if I could have quieted my static before speaking with them, I could have done a much better job of addressing the need for supervision in a way that extended their learning rather than causing them to respond with defensiveness."

Extend Learning Strategy One: Focus on Goals You Set Together

How often have you thought or heard another coach say, "My goals for a teacher are . . ." or something like "She isn't really focusing on my goals"?

Clarissa, who is from Arkansas, was willing to share a sentiment that many coaches have expressed:

> I am working on an old habit of skirting around the topic of goals. I now know that I did this because I wasn't sure what the teacher wanted to work on, what she thought our relationship was for, or if she would be open to my suggestions. The grace in my journey to become more effective as a coach has come as a result of writing things down before I talk with a teacher—making intentional plans about what to say and how to say it. By developing a written plan for our conversation, I can be sure to give the teacher space to participate in the conversation. I can be sure to use specific strengths-based feedback.

Interactions in the work place should enhance everyone's thinking. For this to occur there must be a shift from a "culture of teaching" to a "culture of learning" (DuFour 2004). In Peter Senge's seminal work, *The Fifth Discipline*, he describes a learning organization as a culture

> where people continually expand their capacity to create the results they truly desire, where new and expansive patterns of thinking are nurtured, where collective aspiration is set free, and where people are continually learning to see the whole together. (1990, 3)

As a coach, you may have goals for changes you hope to see in a teacher's practice or classroom. These may come from classroom observations, formal program assessments, or directives from the program supervisor. The process of goal setting often gets stuck here because while the goals are set out, the

Tychawn shares insights about setting goals. Video #18. Go to powerfulinteractions.com/ coachingbook to access this video.

teacher may not see their importance, may disagree with them, or may have other priorities she wants to attend to first.

In Powerful Interactions coaching, we differentiate between "your" goals for a teacher and the goals you and a teacher set together. Sometimes they are the same. Other times you may have to put some of your goals on hold or modify them to meet the best interests and needs of your learning partner.

The goals you set **with** a teacher provide a shared focus that creates a sense of ownership and investment for the teacher. This commitment is necessary if she is going to make a meaningful and lasting positive change in her practice.

By appreciating a teacher's current level of competence, coaches value the natural learning processes of those they coach. Encouraging teachers to clarify what they want and need, build on their strengths, and experiment in the service of mutually agreed-upon goals empowers them to take more initiative and responsibility for their own learning and professional development (Tschannen-Moran & Tschannen-Moran 2011a).

Creating shared goals. Think of goal setting as establishing a big picture plan for your work together. For example,

- Wendy wants to help 4-year-olds hear their own voices as learners.
- Jenny wants to help 3-year-olds sustain and extend their own play when the teacher steps away from the action.
- Lucy is grappling with how to delegate responsibility to the other adults in the toddler room.
- Devon is learning how to improve his relationships with the families of the infants in his care.
- Megan is working on positive guidance strategies in her preschool classroom.

Reality Check

When the relationship is not developed as a learning partnership and goals haven't been clearly articulated, the hidden message underlying the conversation may be "Whose agenda is this anyway?" During a conversation, the teacher may be thinking, When will this be over? The coach may be thinking, Why is this teacher so resistant? In this situation, it is vital to do what our colleague, Helena, calls a "relationship reset." She suggests that you say, "Something isn't working between us. Let's see if we can get back on course."

Helena talks about the importance of acknowledging tension between herself and a teacher and how she moves forward to repair the relationship. Video #19. Go to powerfulinteractions.com/coachingbook to access this video.

These big picture plans were established through conversations between coach and teacher. They began by the coach observing in the teacher's setting and noticing strengths the teacher demonstrated. By describing and sharing the strengths the coach had noticed, and then being quiet so that the teacher could respond, the coach created a space for the teacher to describe aspects of her teaching that are important to her.

Sarah shares what she is learning about "I notice" statements. Video #20. Go to powerfulinteractions.com/coachingbook to access this video.

For Sarah Leibert, a coach in Connecticut, it began when she noticed that Wendy had displayed photographs of children at work along with their products. Sarah was thinking how great it would be if Wendy added the children's dictation to the display. Rather than telling her that, Sarah paused to let Wendy respond and Wendy talked extensively about how much she cares about giving children a voice. This was a perfect opening for Sarah to talk about next steps for Wendy.

Coaches who have had success working with teachers on shared goals describe many different ways the goals emerge:

- A teacher brings an idea to the table. As Monica states, "My role as a coach is to help teachers articulate the goals and return to those goals over time to keep them relevant. Often, I will simply ask teachers to talk about something they want to keep in mind in their teaching, and usually what they describe is a goal that we can focus on during coaching."

- You notice something the teacher would benefit from focusing on and you guide her into a discussion about it. Clarissa describes how she guided Megan's interest in creating a more peaceful classroom toward establishing focused goals related to setting up systems to help children develop greater independence and self-regulation skills.

- Together you review and analyze findings from data gathered either from a program assessment or child outcomes assessments as you consider what is best for the children.

- A program adopts a new health and nutrition curriculum and teachers request specific guidance after initial professional development activities.

Coaching with Powerful Interactions

Periodically offer a reminder about your role and that of the teacher. You might restate that the teacher's interests, needs, and questions determine your shared agenda. The focus of your work is to support her in creating a high-quality program for children and families. Then explain that you are collaborating in a learning partnership and you each have much to learn from the other.

Use your coaching stance and apply a strengths-based perspective. Invite the teacher to talk about something she feels confident about in her classroom and suggest that you might observe and photograph these moments so that together you can analyze how they work so well. "Let's think together about the times of the day that children are deeply engaged in learning."

Focus on goals: Stories from the field. Diana shares this story that illustrates it can take time to fine-tune a goal with a teacher:

> At our first meeting, I asked Ms. Green, "What do you have in mind for our goals?" She wanted to focus on asking children open-ended questions. She also mentioned needing help with transitions.
>
> I went to her classroom to observe. I didn't see anything about transitions that was a problem. She was very skilled. It didn't take long to figure out that she was simply looking for some additional ideas to add to her already rich collection of transition strategies.
>
> Her first comment about open-ended questions was something we kept coming back to in our work, so I watched for that when I observed her classroom. One day I realized that she was good at formulating questions. The piece that was missing was a back-and-forth conversation after children responded. For example, she'd ask, "Why do you think the bubbles popped?" When a child responded, "Too much soap," she said, "OK" and moved on to her next question without saying, "Tell me more about that" or "Why do you think that might be so?" I had been trying so hard to practice finding moments of effectiveness that I missed focusing on our goal. Only when I did could I support her in clarifying it. Only then were we able to think and talk about it together.

Manage Your Time

One half hour is long enough for a coaching feedback session. Meetings longer than 30 minutes increase the chances you will end up going in three or four directions rather than focusing together on a single goal.

Danielle shares a story about how sometimes a teacher might meet one of her goals in some areas of the classroom and need a little support to take what she already knows and does to meet her goal across all areas.

> When we did a goals survey at the beginning of the year, one of the teachers I coach told me that she wanted to work on incorporating more math and literacy opportunities in the learning centers. So I set up my first visit during center time. In some centers she'd done a great job of incorporating both math and literacy. In others there were no signs of either one. When we met, I shared strengths-based feedback about those in which she had already met her goal.
>
> That allowed her to realize and then share with me that she was having a difficult time coming up with math and literacy ideas for the other centers. So we brainstormed ideas for those centers together.

Diana talks about how accountability is a two-way street. Video #21. Go to powerfulinteractions.com/coachingbook to access this video.

 Reality Check

Be transparent about your role. The coach–teacher relationship is not a personal relationship but rather a collaboration with shared purpose on behalf of children and families. Each partner has something important to contribute. Each is accountable to the other in reaching the goals.

The following email correspondence between Jessica (a coach) and Karen (who teaches 4-year-olds) shows how Jessica intentionally highlights goals in her follow-up and creates a way to continue the conversation, strengthening the focus on goals and increasing the chances of meeting them:

Dear Karen,

Thank you for welcoming me in your classroom last week! When we spoke you mentioned your goal is to focus on language and literacy skills, specifically emergent writing and print concepts. Let's focus our next visit on this. Please send me a quick email outlining the opportunities you already provide children to recognize/"read" print in their classroom environment and write for a purpose, and where you would like support. This will help us use the time efficiently. I will be at your program on Thursday the 23rd. When you send the email with emergent reading and writing information, please let me know what time Thursday afternoon is best for us to meet.

Jessica

Dear Jessica,

My focus is on emergent writing and print concepts. The preschoolers in my class are ready to practice writing—at a level that is appropriate for their skills and stage of development. I expose them to print in multiple settings. For example, we use a daily sign-in sheet, and have introduced their last names to the list. This has meaning for some but not all of the children. We also use illustrated vocabulary cards that are posted around the classroom pertaining to the current exploration. This helps them learn that the print and pictures go together. As we talk about the cards, they begin to understand that print carries meaning. I have found that writing is more difficult for some because they are still developing the fine motor skills needed to hold and use writing tools. I offer lots of fine motor activities to help children naturally build the small muscles used for drawing and writing.

Reflections

Some of the coaches we have talked with who are using Powerful Interactions have realized that they were not setting goals. They simply expected teachers to do so, and then felt frustrated when the teachers did not stick with the goals they set for themselves. As a coaching team, they decided to set some goals for themselves and for the division and revisit them regularly. This has helped them see from the teachers' perspective that it helps when goals are stated clearly and there is follow-up to discuss progress and next steps.

Another group of coaches realized that their attention was focused on what was happening in the moment in their work with teachers leading them to making links to the goals previously discussed. They committed to try to take notes and use them as a reference in future conversations with teachers. By reviewing their notes, they could talk about insights from previous sessions, which helped coach and teacher deepen their exploration and understanding of a topic.

Do you set personal goals? If yes, pause to think about them. What role do they play in your daily life? How do you monitor your progress?

Do you have goals for yourself as a coach? If yes, pause to think about them. What role do they play in your daily work life? How do you monitor your progress in your growth and development as a coach?

We discussed different ways to incorporate print and writing in other classroom environments that may be of more interest to the children. I plan to try some these ideas.

It is important as well to expose the children to the print all around them. This can be something as simple as just pointing it out or providing pictures of recognizable print in their environment. You brought in a toothpaste box. Thank you. It is a good example of text children will recognize and provides additional print in the classroom. I plan to bring in other boxes of items and foods that are familiar to the children to include in the dramatic play area.

We also discussed the different stages of writing each child may be at. This is an area in which continued support will be helpful for me and the children I teach. We can continue to discuss these topics when we meet. I am available anytime on Thursday afternoon. Feel free to stop in whenever it is convenient for you.

Thank you, Jessica.

Karen

Tips for focusing on goals. If a goal is clear and specific, it is more likely that you and a teacher can focus on working together to address it:

- Be explicit. Define goals, actions steps, outcomes, and timelines. Shortly before the end of a feedback session or in an email prior to the next visit, raise the question of goals. You might say, "How are we doing with regard to the goal we set a few weeks back? How would you describe your progress? Do you want to keep this focus, narrow it down, or shift to another goal?" Take some time to decide together. When you come to an agreement, write it down for both of you. This sets the stage for the fourth Extend Learning strategy that you will read about later, "Document Plans and Progress." As coach, it is your job to follow up with an email or text reminding the teacher of the goal that you agreed upon, what steps you are both taking, and by when.

Clarissa and Jeanne clarify plans to work together. Video #22.
Go to powerfulinteractions.com/coachingbook to access this video.

- Make sure the steps to meet the goal are manageable. An important part of goal setting is recognizing what is involved in achieving the goal. For example, if a teacher says that she wants to focus on small groups, this is the perfect time to ask, "Let's think about small group time. What strengths do you bring to small group?" If the teacher can list some, great. If not, perhaps your first observation is to notice her moments of effectiveness and help her to articulate what she does well and why it matters. Then you might say, "Let's think about these things you do well. Can they serve you in other ways during small group time? Let's think about when the children were most engaged. What were you doing to make that happen? When did their engagement wane? Let's think together about what you might have done differently to sustain their level of engagement."

- Follow up and encourage follow through. Jaquie shares what she has learned: "I try to be conscientious about following up and asking how something's working. If I don't, I find that each time I come to the site, we are on to the crisis of the day. If we shift directions every time, it undermines my sense of being effective and the teacher's too." To keep the momentum going with a goal, coaches use emails, text messages, and phone calls to make sure that the steps are taken. Clarissa invites teachers to send her a photo of what they have done and how children are responding to the change.

  Clarissa sent this note to Megan right after a visit to her classroom: "Megan, I'm eager to hear how children are responding to the choice board you were going to post. Please send a photo of children using it!" A few days later Megan texted a photo and a brief note (see exchange to the right).

- Restate the goal each time you meet to maintain a shared focus. If you are visiting the classroom to observe, reference the goal in your reminder email: "I'm looking forward to visiting your classroom this Thursday at 11:00. In our last conversation we agreed that you would be working on incorporating mathematical thinking into transitions. I'll be sure to take notes so that we can talk about what you try and how children respond." When you arrive in the classroom, quiet your static and remember the focus of your visit.

- Look for moments of effectiveness that are small steps towards the goal. For example, a teacher is struggling with leading music and movement activities that engage the

Clarissa texted Megan right after a visit to her classroom and the conversation continued back and forth.

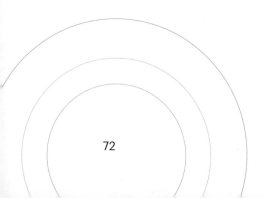

Documenting the Story of the Teacher's Work

The coach's role is to lead the process of documenting the teacher's progress along the journey of meeting a goal. It begins with the two of you writing down the goal you set together. This means working with the teacher to choose items and create a collection of observations, insights, photographs that together make it possible for a teacher to see and talk about what she has learned and see positive change in her practice over time.

children. During your observation, you notice several missteps on the part of the teacher. Quiet your static about those first. Notice what she is doing effectively with regard to leading the activity. Later on, when you meet with the teacher, describe the impact it has on children. Then say, "Let's think together if that effective strategy could have served you at any other point during the morning."

- **Review what has come before.** This helps you to support the teacher in seeing her progress (and you'll feel a sense of satisfaction too). As we said earlier, teachers are busy and an important role you can play in their professional lives is to document their progress and help them make connections in their work. Some coaches use tablets or computers to document their sessions. Others have forms. Some use notebooks. Whatever method you use, it is important to show the teacher that you are looking back on what came before and helping him see his progress over time. This is an important way to model teaching behaviors that support children's learning.

- **Link coaching goals to other required goal setting.** In many settings, teachers and providers have required goals for their programs, including teacher evaluation goals or school improvement goals. To support teachers, connect the work they do with you—their coach—with other requirements they have to address. For example, Jaquie was coaching a teacher of 4-year-olds whose district "smart goal" was focused on literacy outcomes. While the smart goal was very specific, they decided to make the focus of their coaching work teaching strategies related to children's literacy outcomes. This was their broad focus. They began by thinking about ways to enrich each learning center with books and other texts.

Extend Learning Strategy Two: Notice Moments of Effectiveness

We believe that every person has strengths and moments of effectiveness. When the coach offers strengths-based feedback to a teacher, she provides the effective practice (like a mirror for the teacher) and explains the positive impact the teacher's actions or language have on the children.

Highlighting moments of effectiveness will look different from one person to another. In the photo on the right, for example, you might highlight the addition of the book or the magnifiers or the posted conversation prompts on the wall. As you read the following examples of articulating moments of effectiveness to foster intentionality and professional growth, consider how they address individual strengths:

- A director said that saying to a competent teacher, "I see you labeled your shelves with words and pictures and that helps children learn to match the word with a picture" does not recognize the teacher's knowledge and skills. Instead, she chose to say, "I see you intentionally labeled your shelves with words and pictures. I'm interested to hear about this decision and how the children are responding."

- A coach highlights a teacher's competence and invites reflection about intentionality: "I noticed that during the morning activities from center time through cleanup, hand washing, and lunch, children were busy and productive. Children demonstrated initiative, and they worked together to accomplish tasks. Talk about your decision making, your goals for children's learning, and how you teach children to be so independent."

- A coach sets the stage for a future conversation about a few areas of the classroom that need changes to the type of materials and how they are organized: "Children were deeply engaged in the art area today, using materials inventively and talking with each other about their creations. The way you taped the paper to the table allowed the toddlers to explore with materials freely and paint over the entire paper with a sense of competence."

For a teacher who rarely smiles, needs lots of support creating a warm climate in the classroom, and doesn't respond favorably to suggestions, spend time in the classroom and document her infrequent smiles with two or three photos. Then catch her expressing warmth! Bring the photos to a conversation and say, "Carla, when you smile your eyes light up. This lets the

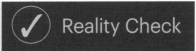

children know you care about them and are interested in what they do. Notice how Rayna is looking back at you, eager to have your attention!"

In Powerful Interactions coaching, moments of effectiveness are stepping stones that create a path between where a teacher is and where he can be as he works with you to enhance his practice (Lopez & Louis 2009). As you identify and call attention to these moments using "I notice" statements, you strengthen your relationship and give a teacher the information he needs to intentionally enhance an area of his practice.

Using "I notice" statements is one place where we offer a suggestion to help coaches get started: "I notice that you _____. This is important because _____." Of course, you can personalize your message. What matters is describing a specific teaching behavior and the impact it has on child's learning and development.

Many coaches have asked us if they have to use "I notice" statements with every teacher all the time. The answer of course is no. We do believe, however, that noticing someone's moments of effectiveness and calling attention to their importance is a way to connect with and validate the work of the other person.

Although it may sound simple, finding moments of effectiveness to highlight with "I notice" statements can be challenging. It takes "getting over yourself" (remember Judy's story?). Diana remembers: "I once observed in a classroom with a frog theme. It didn't bother anybody but me. I had to get past it so I could look at the children, teachers, and interactions."

In addition, many coaches say that they do not have the knowledge or vocabulary to be able to provide helpful "I notice" statements, which impacts their ability to model and promote articulation. It's helpful to work with colleagues to develop the skills you need. It takes ongoing, continuous practice.

Sarah shares what she is learning about "I notice" statements. Video #23. Go to powerfulinteractions.com/coachingbook to access this video.

This is where *Powerful Interactions: How to Connect with Children to Extend Their Learning* can support you. The chapters on Connect and Extend Learning strategies are filled with language and ideas you can use as you model and promote articulation during professional conversations.

Using "I notice" statements: Stories from the field. We all need to feel competent. When you notice the moments of effectiveness and highlight them using "I notice" statements, you help teachers focus on what they are doing well. This helps give them the confidence and motivation to continue doing what is working.

We recently received an email from Catharina, a colleague in New York City, who is just learning to use "I notice" statements in her program. Here's what she said:

> Hello all,
>
> I made two "I notice" statements yesterday, one to a teacher and one to our school safety agent. The first one I practiced saying in my head before I opened my mouth and the other just came out.
>
> 1) I noticed that when you shared that story with Ms. Caesar she felt comforted and reassured.
>
> 2) I noticed you have learned a lot of our students' and parents' names. That makes our families feel safe and cared for.
>
> In both instances the person receiving the observation was so happy and appreciated the information.
>
> Thank you.
> Catharina

Tips for using "I notice" statements. Use "I notice" statements or find your own words. The main thing is to use specific and concise language that reflects back a teacher's moment of effectiveness and tells her why it is important to a child or children. Whatever words you choose to use, we hope some of these tips will be helpful.

- Train yourself to see through the distractions so you can observe for strengths. Diana shares: "It helps me to see moments of effectiveness when

Reflections

Knowing what pushes your buttons will help you to quiet the static and notice someone's strengths. Many coaches have shared with us that clutter is a hot button. When they walk into a classroom, it is hard for them to get past the clutter and see a teacher's strength. Take a moment to think about the hot buttons that might interfere with you focusing on strengths.

In this video Diana explains that anything, including frogs and environmental clutter, can cause static. Video #24. Go to powerfulinteractions.com/coachingbook to access this video.

Taking notes helps Michael remember what he observes and lets teachers know that he is focused on them and their work. Video #25. Go to powerfulinteractions.com/coachingbook to access this video.

I see something and wish it could be different. Then I peel away the layers to try to understand: Is it important to the child's learning? Established as best practice? I can give the teacher much better feedback if I can figure out not only what is important but why it is important."

- Write down your statements before offering them as feedback. It is almost impossible to come up with clear and specific observations and impact statements without recording them on paper or digitally. We strongly encourage you to record your "I notice" statements so that you can provide clear feedback. Moreover, showing a teacher that you have actually documented a factual observation of her is even more validating than saying it aloud. It models for her the importance of documenting children's learning.

  - Take objective notes during classroom visits. Record factual statements about what you see and hear. Danielle shares: "The notes will help keep you from focusing on one thing too much and possibly miss something (positive or negative). Later on you can sort it all out and do away with judgments that clouded your lens while observing. I look for at least two positive things to point out and no more than two things to "work on." Remembering that everyone is good at something can help you keep an open mind when transcribing and reviewing your notes as you prepare for a meeting with a teacher."

- Send validating emails. Jill, a principal in an early childhood program, came up with this method that works for her. As she does her walk-throughs to say good morning each day, she jots down the teacher's name and a strength that she observes. When she returns to her office, she adds why it matters and sends it off to the teacher as a validating email. Over the course of a week, she tries to send one brief validating email to each teacher.

- Be specific. The more specific you are when you describe an effective practice, the more likely the teacher will be able to replicate it. For example, Mr. Josephs says to a teacher in a Head Start program, "You posted children's names and their photos just below their paintings. This helps the 3-year-olds see that their work is valued and they begin to recognize their names in print."

Coaching with Powerful Interactions

- Link the "what" you notice to "why" it is important. There are many ways to do this, depending on the focus of your work with teachers. You can connect your feedback to a specific assessment or to Quality Rating and Improvement Systems (QRIS) instruments.

- Promote intentional decision making based on goals for children's growth and development. "Let's think about your cooking area. What do we want children to do here? What do we want them to learn? How do we want them to feel? What attitudes do we want to cultivate?"

- Use photos or videos to focus on specifics. When coaches and teachers look at photos and watch videos together, the coach can encourage the teacher to notice the specific, effective actions she does and the words she says that support a child's learning.

- Encourage teachers to notice too. As learning partners, your work can only be enriched if the teacher is building his skills at noticing his moments of effectiveness as well. A coach shared that she does this by intentionally inviting teachers to hone in on the specifics of observations they share with her: "If a teacher tells me about a child who was particularly focused on an activity, I encourage the teacher to think about and put into words what the child did that was different and how he might promote this behavior again."

- Resist opinions and judgment. If you say, "That was a great way to end the group meeting," you haven't helped the teacher learn what it is she did. By describing the specific action you see and attaching it to the impact, you eliminate judgment and, at the same time, you validate a practice. So instead you might say, "You ended the group meeting by inviting children to take a minute to think about the center they want to choose, and who they might want to work with. This created a smooth transition for children and supported the development of the executive function skill of planning—deciding what they will do next and who they might do it with."

- Steer clear of a laundry list. No one can hear all of the items on a laundry list. We typically tune out after the first few items. Point out one or two strengths you noticed and the impact they had on the child. As Jackie says, "Focusing on fewer

Time Management

During a classroom observation, you may not have the time to think through how the teacher's decisions impact children's learning. So while observing, jot a few notes to remind you of moments of effectiveness you notice specifically related to the focus of your work together. For example, you simply record:

- Used words: construction, structure, and skyscraper

When you leave the classroom and take some time to prepare for the feedback conversation, you can craft the second part of your "I notice" statement—why the moment of effectiveness is important for children's learning—to address specific goals you have set with the teacher. For example, with the note above, Ms. Shellie, a teacher of 4-year-olds, is working on using language to extend children's thinking and vocabulary. You might write a note that says: "I noticed that when children were building with blocks, you incorporated the words construction, structure and skyscraper as you engaged in conversation with them. This helps children hear and use rich vocabulary."

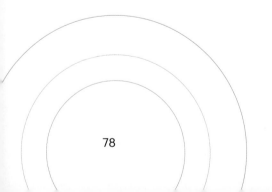

things is making me more effective in having conversations. Once I narrowed my focus and had two-way conversations (I didn't know I wasn't doing that), the teacher felt more comfortable texting, emailing, and talking with me. She is now talking more during study group. She told me, 'You never asked me anything, just told me lots of things.' Now we have two-way conversations."

Extend Learning Strategy Three: Use Prompts and Questions to Think Together

Do you ever catch yourself slipping into "fix-it" mode? Seeing something you would like a teacher to do differently, then generously offering your advice for how to do it? Or perhaps listening to someone's concern and then trying to tell him how to address it?

Coaches we have been talking with say it sounds very familiar. It does to us, too. Irene writes that as she continues to learn about Powerful Interactions coaching, she is "working on talking less and doing more thoughtful questioning and listening." That is the essence of this strategy.

Prompts and questions: Stories from the field. Danielle shares this story of how asking a teacher questions rather than suggesting answers gave the teacher the opportunity to explore, articulate, and deepen her understanding of strategies to engage children in different aspects of pretend play.

I recently talked with Sophia, a kindergarten teacher. Although she is quite reflective, I could tell that she was struggling to support creative play for children who needed help to develop their dramatic play skills. I invited Sophia to talk about specific actions and words she uses when in the dramatic play area. She responded in detail about how she focused the play by taking on the role of cashier at the grocery, asked children questions about what they were buying and what they were going to cook when they got home. She offered shopping bags for them to collect the items to bring their groceries home. By talking it through, she became more aware of how she could offer simple prompts to help children focus their play and use their imaginations. Sophia also mentioned that the boys were not engaged in dramatic play. I asked, "How could the boys be more engaged?" She thought for a moment, then said that she could try to incorporate some of the boys' interests (building, cars, etc.) into props and materials in the area. We then brainstormed ideas she could try. As a result of her increased intentionality, Sophia noticed that over time the children's play grew more complex.

Sometimes prompts and questions lead to jointly considering and solving a problem around program management issues. Diana shares this story of how prompts and questions allowed a director to come up with a plan for fire drills even when the director is not there.

> Kathy, an early childhood program director, was talking with me about how to make sure weekly fire drills would be conducted even when she was not there. She said she'd write "fire drill" on the calendar so everyone would know when it should be.
>
> I thought a moment and asked, "What is the purpose of the fire drill?"
>
> "So everyone will know what do if there is a fire," she replied.
>
> I started saying, "So, if the fire drill is on the calendar and everyone knows about it . . .
>
> She finished my sentence: "Then people will be prepared."
>
> I could see her thinking and sat there quietly. She then went on to say, "Maybe I don't want everyone to know when it is going to be." The solution she came up with: Use the program management software to let people in the office know to schedule a fire drill, and keep the reminder there for the week until the drill is held.

Diana shares an insight that has helped her frame questions. Video #26. Go to powerfulinteractions.com/coachingbook to access this video.

Tips for prompts and questions. As you use prompts and questions in your interactions with a teacher, the words you say will often become part of the conversation a teacher has with herself and with colleagues about her practice. This has the potential to deepen her understanding and enrich her practice. Here are some tips that can help you make prompts and questions an intentional part of your coaching:

- Use prompts and questions to invite reflection and back-and-forth conversation:
    - I'm curious. How do my observations compare to your own?
    - During this learning experience what worked well for you? What worked well for the children? Why do you think so?

Sometimes prompts and questions lead to thinking and problem solving for adults. Video #27. Go to powerfulinteractions.com/coachingbook to access this video.

- Tell me more about _____.
- Let's think about why that happened.
- Let's think about another way that you could use that strategy to _____.
- Is there something you've tried in another situation that might have worked here?
- I wonder why children _____. What are your thoughts about that?
- Change "tells" to "asks":
    - I'm interested in how or why _____?
    - Tell me more about _____.
    - How did you decide to _____?
- Ask about the teacher's decision making. Especially when working with an experienced teacher, demonstrate respect by inviting her to talk about her thinking and decision-making. You might start a conversation by noticing that the children made many interesting observations during their nature walk. Ask her to talk about the decisions she's made to help children enjoy and learn from their outdoor experiences.
- Before offering a strategy, ask the teacher if she would like a suggestion. Diana shares this idea: "Sometimes a teacher will mention that she isn't sure how to do something. That's my cue. I'll ask, 'Would you be interested in hearing what I've seen other teachers try?' or 'I have some ideas about that, if you'd like to hear them.' In this way, I express respect for the teacher as a learner and allow her to ask for ideas."

Sarah shares her discovery that pausing gives teachers time they need to think and demonstrates her trust in them. Video #28. Go to powerfulinteractions.com/coachingbook to access this video.

Coaching with Powerful Interactions

- Solve problems together. In the conversation on page 79, Diana asked a question then gave a director time to think. This gave her space, time, and a little guidance, something we all need at times to find a solution. This models how to solve a problem as partners.

Extend Learning Strategy Four: Document Plans and Progress Together

For a long time, we have understood the power of documentation. Amy's work for much of her career has been documenting stories of change at the program and state level. Both Judy and Amy have worked and written about documenting children's learning for more than 20 years, and in the past 10 years Shaun has joined us in using video to document teachers' work. As we worked on this guide, we heard repeatedly about how the coaching relationship is challenged by the absence of meaningful record keeping. Most coaches say that the required paperwork feels burdensome and is focused on their accountability. What we are introducing in this section is a process of documenting the story of the coach and teacher's work done in partnership and in an individualized style that works for teacher and coach, strengthens their relationship, and moves their work ahead. There are many ways to record this documentation—written on a steno pad or entered into a tablet or computer. One person may have a running document on her laptop while the other may have a folder of photos and written notes.

We believe that this process of documentation addresses all three steps of a Powerful Interaction:

- Be Present. Prior to an exchange ideally both participants take a moment to look back at their notes, review the current goals, and think about the focus of the exchange. In fact, as the coach, it is your responsibility to initiate this first step. This is your job: to pause and be present, to get you and the teacher on the same page in a steadying and static-quieting way. Pausing to prepare in this way focuses you and quiets your static so that you, in turn, can do the same for the teacher.

- Connect. Ongoing written communication is a way to build trust and deepen your relationship. Sending a quick text or email, such as "I'm looking forward to observing group time this afternoon," connects you. It lets the teacher know you see her and focuses on your work.

Reality Check

Coaches often feel uncomfortable coming up with the right questions and prompts for each teacher. To support the principles of learning partnerships and individualizing, invite teachers to think about questions and prompts you can ask that would engage them and support their thinking and learning. We recently had the opportunity to do this at a staff meeting with teachers at Wintonbury Early Childhood Magnet School. We thank them for letting us share some of their thoughts. The following are their suggestions for questions and prompts:

- Do you feel validated? How?

- What are your strengths?

- Where do you want to grow? How can I help you?

- What are you passionate about? In school and life?

- What do you want to share with others?

- How and when can we follow up?

- Can you help me see this situation from your perspective?

- How can we work together to take these ideas deeper?

Helena describes the many ways a coach and teacher can document their work together. Video #29. Go to powerfulinteractions.com/coachingbook to access this video.

- Extend Learning. Now let's think about how documentation Extends Learning, the third step of a Powerful Interaction. Writing things down—documentation—allows you to step back and clarify your thinking. In the coach–teacher relationship, rather than simply relying on conversation and memory, you move the learning ahead by using documentation to capture the story of your work together. This includes writing down

  - Your shared goals and plans

  - Specific actions and responsibilities you each commit to

  - Examples of the teacher's moments of effectiveness and the impact they have on children's learning

  - Questions you discuss together

  - New ideas you want to explore

  When you and a teacher are so busy and experience everyday static, it can be difficult to see and hear the story of a teacher's progress and change. You can support the teacher by initiating this process of documentation and then figuring out together how to keep it going. It is the story that can allow you both to see where you have been, recognize your many accomplishments, and make intentional decisions about the next steps you will take to meet your shared goals.

  Documenting keeps you focused on goals. Laura Lamothe, a coach supervisor in Arizona, talks about how easy it is to go from visit to visit without a focus, hearing about the current crisis or success of the day, and more often than not, personal stories that may strengthen the relationship but fail to move the work ahead. She says, "Documenting what you are doing together keeps you focused on the goals and on course."

  When the coaching relationship begins and you have established a focus for the work, it is important that both you and the teacher agree upon your plan for working together. Record this plan so that you can return to it on a regular basis.

  Documentation supports accountability and reciprocity. Both you and the teacher are busy, and it's easy to forget things if you don't write them down. Having an established plan and habit of recording your work together helps you stay accountable to each other for your professional responsibilities. It ensures that your work goes beyond what can be a warm and comforting conversational relationship. The shared record of your work helps you to stay accountable to your role in supporting the teacher's professional growth. It supports the teacher in moving ahead and becoming more consciously competent in her practice (that is, building her strengths).

The documentation allows you to check in together and respond to questions such as

- Have we done an effective job summarizing the outcome of our conversation?
- Are we walking away with same messages?
  - What is your take-away?
  - What is my take-away?
- How are we going to follow up?
- What are we each going to do and by when?
- How can we support each other?
- How should we check in with each other and when?

Laura says, "If I don't document, I don't trust it will happen."

Documentation sustains ongoing conversation. Maintaining two-way communication between coaching visits allows your work to keep moving ahead, even when you are not face-to-face. This deepens the reciprocity of your professional relationship. It matters how you shape these emails and what you ask for. For example, when Clarissa asked Megan to send a picture of children using the choice board, she immediately got a message back with an enthusiastic note from Megan. That allowed Clarissa to respond to the picture with an "I notice" statement validating Megan's efforts.

Clarissa says,

I try to maintain regular communication with teachers between the times we see each other in person. Sometimes I'll send an interesting quote and article, reflection questions, or other resources. Even when I send a group email to several teachers, I believe it supports my relationships with teachers and moves our work together forward.

Documentation reveals progress and change over time. Documentation helps you and the teacher look back and reflect on the story of the teacher's growing wisdom over time. Together you can see where you have been and the steps that have been taken to reach this point. It creates an opportunity for validation and celebration of the work you have done together. Knowing where you have been and where you want to go leads to intentional decision making about new goals and next steps.

Keep the conversation going: Stories from the field.

Diana shares the following experience about taking notes and summarizing conversations.

> During a feedback conversation with Flora, who teaches 4-year-olds, I say, "I'm interested in the rocks. . . ." Flora talks about the rocks and the arrangement.
>
> **The brief notes I take as we talk**
>
> - Collecting rocks
> - Variations
> - Looking for pictures—river rocks, rock formations
> - Children could duplicate
> - Paint rocks—textures
> - Explore over time
>
> I say, "Have you noticed how the children used the rocks during the year?" (or similar question or statement). We talk about what Flora noticed the children doing.
>
> **The notes I take as we continue to talk**
>
> - Dump, but not really looking
> - Only a few weeks
> - Exploration
>
> I say, "You thought the children might bring in rocks to add to the collection, but they haven't. Let's think together about how to invite contributions to the rocks center. . . ." (or similar question or statement). Flora shares ideas for engaging children in collecting rocks to add to the center.

The notes I take as the conversation continues

- Look outside

- Talk where

Thoughts about writing notes during the conversation

- I tried to use Judy's suggestion of recording verbs as Flora described her rocks center. In the moment, it was easy to look at my notes and reflect back to her the steps she took to design the rocks center.

- In a future conversation, the description of her design steps might serve as the foundation for thinking about redesigning one of the other centers. Having a written record of the design steps would support that conversation.

- Writing down only what Flora said helped me be present and listen more effectively. I did not write any "notes to self" at that time—only what I was hearing.

Reviewing the notes a week later

- Although bits of the conversation were fuzzy, my notes about what Flora said were enough to help me reflect on possibilities for our continued work together.

- As I looked at the documentation of the feedback conversation with Flora, I noted that the "look" of the page with a photo and the typed notes demonstrates the importance and value I place on the conversation, specifically on Flora's thoughts and ideas. Recording only what Flora said clearly shows that the focus is on her experience.

Reflecting on my notes

- When reflecting on my notes, I celebrated some of my moments of effectiveness in that conversation: listening carefully; mirror talk (providing words to help Flora think more deeply about what she had described); trying to replace expert language with coaching language.

- Reflecting on my notes and my moments of effectiveness as a coach caused me to think about the strategies I want to continue to use so that they become coaching habits (see celebrated moments above).

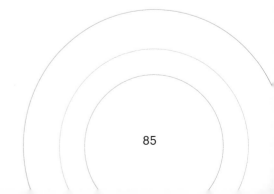

Manage Your Time

Documentation should not become a project that either of you have to do in your spare time. Writing a few sentences or a few phrases regularly or taking a photo and adding a caption add up over time. In addition to supporting your learning partnership, the teacher, when applicable, can use the documentation you create together to support her own professional portfolio.

• Rereading my notes about writing notes (see p. 84), I realized that my goal for Flora was for her to redesign the other centers in the classroom. Her goal was to find ways to facilitate deeper and broader engagement with the rocks—and her ideas were good ones! My goal of redesigning centers was for the purpose of enriching children's learning experience (and maybe a little about how the room looked to me). Flora's goal of continuing to engage children with rocks was for the purpose of enriching children's learning experience. Two different goals with the same purpose—that's how I can let go of my preferences and support the teacher's goal. The end result will be the same—rich learning experiences for children. As I thought more about it, there was still much that could be done with the rocks center. Had I suggested that Flora turn her attention to another center, it might have been as ineffective as trying to guide a child to leave dramatic play before he is finished so that he can experience all the centers.

• The importance of a written record of the coaching experience for the teacher and for the coach is clear to me. Look how much I learned from documenting the 5- to 10-minute feedback conversation! I learned things that will help me be more effective as a coach so that Flora can be more effective in her practice.

• I wonder what would happen if I asked Flora to record key words and phrases from the conversation (after the conversation)? She could write as much or as little as she wished. In the next visit (and via email between visits), we plan to compare our records of the conversation and our reflections. For some teachers this might be torture, but for some it might become an important strategy or tool for guiding one's own professional growth.

Tips for documenting plans and progress.

- Individualize. Talk about methods of documenting that will work for each of you. They don't have to match. You may want to use your tablet and the teacher may keep a folder with papers and photos.

- Keep it simple. The most important aspect of documentation is that it exists, not how fancy it is! You each need a manageable method that you can sustain and refer back to over time. For example, Michael keeps a notebook and pen in his shirt pocket.

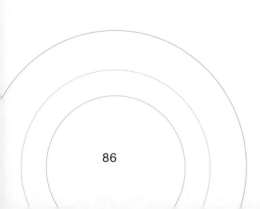

Coaching with Powerful Interactions

- Summarize conversations. Your role during observations and conversations is to keep track of key ideas so that you can summarize the conversation for the teacher. One strategy that some coaches are experimenting with is writing key verbs that a teacher says during conversations (read Diana's story that begins on p. 84). This allows you to draw out strategies that the teacher is describing and then you can reflect them back to her as her wisdom.

- Encourage teachers to share their challenges, successes, and lessons learned with their colleagues. Support teachers' efforts to talk about their experiences at staff meetings, write about them in a program newsletter, present at a conference, contribute an entry to the Powerful Interactions Facebook page, or write an article for a journal or magazine.

- Use emails between visits to offer additional "I notice" statements. You may drop by a teacher's classroom between formal coaching visits and notice a moment of effectiveness. If you do, jot it down and send it to the teacher to validate her practice. This takes just a few minutes but can have a big impact on the teacher's sense of professionalism.

- Use photos and video for documentation. Photos and video clips are a terrific way to capture moments of the teacher's effectiveness and to let the teacher see herself in action. They ensure specificity and focus and keep the conversation factual. They serve as a mirror, a tool for conversation. We have referred to them as a teacher's "instant replay."

> Documenting contributes to articulation, individualization, and the learning partnership. Whether it's a journal entry, a photo and caption, or a collection of sticky notes, the documentation process includes identifying what happened, why it was important enough to document, how I felt about it, what I learned from it, and questions and things to continue to think about regarding what happened. Every time I document and review a coaching activity, nuances emerge that I had not seen in the moment and that deepen my understanding of the teacher, of myself, of the learning partnership, and of coaching in general. It's intentional, but doesn't have to be formal. If it feels like one more burden added to your shoulders, you're doing it wrong!

Reality Check

We've heard many coaches and teachers resist the idea of documenting their work together because it feels like yet another task to do. We encourage you to give it a try. Let us know how it is going on our Powerful Interactions website or Facebook page where we will post more examples and tips about documentation.

Michael and Dana talk about what it feels like to get an email from a coach supervisor. Video #30. Go to powerfulinteractions.com/coachingbook to access this video.

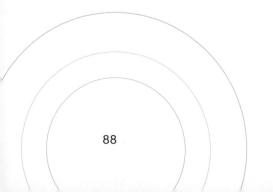

> Experiment until you find the method and time that fit you. It can feel awkward at first. Keep it on your to-do list until it becomes a natural part of your coaching practice.

Diana invites each of us to "experiment until you find the right method and time that fit you." She also says that over time, documentation will become a "natural part of your coaching practice." We believe this is true for each of the strategies we have talked about in this chapter. Conversations that extend a teacher's learning can take place anywhere, anytime: in the classroom, sitting together in your office, even during a brief conversation in the hallway. It is your intentionality as you quiet the static to Be Present, Connect, and Extend Learning using the strategies we have just discussed that transform a casual conversation about work into a Powerful Interaction.

Over time, your practice and that of the teachers who are your learning partners will deepen and your work on behalf of children and families will become even more effective. We turn now to a few final thoughts we'd like to share from some of the people you have met in this book, and we close our conversation by inviting you to build on your strengths as you incorporate Powerful Interactions into your coaching.

Closing Thoughts

Throughout this book you've heard from us and from many colleagues around the country. We hope you have found these ideas informative and inspirational. We'd like to leave you with a few final thoughts.

From Diana: Relationships between coaches and teachers build slowly. When I am consistently noticing moments of effectiveness, it helps the teacher relax and she begins to trust me. She comes to a place where she can say, "Okay, she's not here to get me. She's not going to tell me what I'm doing is wrong."

From Tychawn: For me, using Powerful Interactions in my coaching has pushed me to practice articulating how teachers' actions support children's learning. This allows me to work with teachers in ways that increase their intentionality. My interactions with teachers are now exchanges that go back and forth—they are richer, vibrant, and more alive. This happens when I start conversations with "Oh, I noticed that you did that."

From Michael: Using Powerful Interactions has created a positive trend in my center that has strengthened ALL relationships—between adults and children and between adults.

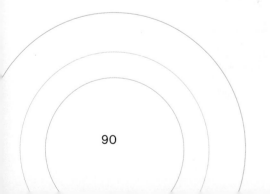

Now we invite you to build on your moments of effectiveness. Take an idea, a principle, a strategy, or a tip that you have found meaningful and make it yours.

Pause, take a breath, and be present as you allow yourself a few minutes to reread a page or two or watch and listen to a video clip. Think about steps you might take to incorporate an aspect of coaching with Powerful Interactions in your daily work.

Perhaps you might begin by taking your own photo or video or by jotting down your thoughts and questions. Above all, engage in Powerful Interactions with colleagues about your practice so that you can continue the conversation.

We invite you to share your stories about the positive ripples you create as you begin coaching with Powerful Interactions. Join the Powerful interactions community by following our blog at powerfulinteractions.com and through Facebook and Twitter.

Judy, Amy, and Shaun

Appendix

Coaching Strategies at-a-Glance

Whether you are having a Powerful Interaction with a teacher during a planned coaching session or in a spontaneous meeting in the hallway, this At-a-Glance Guide can be a helpful reminder of Powerful Interactions steps and strategies.

Step One: Be Present

- Quiet the Static. Adjust to find the "just right fit."

Step Two: Connect

- Be Trustworthy. Be on time. Refer to past conversations and discoveries to recall your shared history of working and learning together.

- Listen to Learn. Ask questions to learn more. Remember everyone brings expertise to the table.

- Communicate to Form a Partnership. Keep the conversation two-way. Pause often for think time and let your partner know you are thinking.

Step Three: Extend Learning

- Focus on Goals. Restate the purpose as you open your meeting. Review the goal you set together.

- Notice Moments of Effectiveness. Use "I notice" statements. Be prepared with a few clear notes identifying the moments of effectiveness you want to highlight. Highlight why the teacher's actions and words are important to teaching and learning. Avoid judgmental or evaluative words ("I liked how you did . . ."). Instead, say

    - I noticed _____.

    - I was watching children do _____.

    - I saw _____ during the transition.

    - I noticed you using _____ as a strategy for _____.

- Use Prompts and Questions to Think Together.
  - Use open-ended questions. Sometimes the phrases "Let's think about . . ." or "I wonder about . . ." or "I'm interested to know more about . . ." invite a conversation more than simply asking, "Why did you do that?" Discussion starters to follow "I notice" statements include
    - I'm curious to know what you observed.
    - During this experience, what worked well for you? Why do you think so?
    - Tell me more about _____.
    - I am interested to know more about your decision to _____.
  - Highlight a strategy the teacher uses "unconsciously" and encourage her to use it with more intention.
  - Encourage him to try a new strategy.
  - Suggest a resource that might be helpful.
  - Offer to model a strategy.
- Document Plans and Progress Together. Invite the educator to summarize the conversation and establish a time frame for completing the next step. Stay in touch. Invite the teacher to email you with a success story. Send her a note of encouragement.

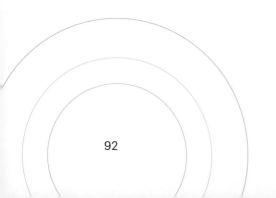

Coaching with Powerful Interactions

A Powerful Interactions Classroom Observation and Feedback Conversation

Classroom Observation

1. Be Present

Preparation (before arriving at the classroom)

- Do a Me Check. Stop and breathe. Assess your static level. If you notice static is present, give yourself a moment to quiet it before moving ahead.
- Review your notes from your last coaching conversation or the notes you prepared for this observation.
- Jot down reminders to keep you focused on the next steps you determined with the teacher.
- Determine which observational tools you plan to use (for example, video, voice recordings, photographs, or notes).

Right before you enter the classroom

- Repeat the Me Check. Quiet any static created between the time you prepared and your arrival.

2. Connect

- Greet the teacher by name. Thank her for welcoming you into her setting.
- Focus on the purpose and plan for the visit when identifying specific examples of teaching and learning strengths.
- Capture the teacher's moments of effectiveness through video, voice recordings, photographs, or notes.
- Be respectful of what is happening in the classroom. Try to be inconspicuous. Whether you are recording or writing notes, be sure to observe the classroom interactions for no more than five minutes at a time.

Feedback Conversation

3. Extend Learning

- Make sure you are present. Be prepared with a few clear notes identifying the moments of effectiveness you want to highlight.

- Open to connect. Thank the teacher for allowing you to visit. Check in to see how she is feeling. Remember to keep up a two-way conversation! Pause often for think time.

- Restate the purpose. Review the goal you set together for this visit.

- Present the observation. Validate the teacher with "I notice" statements. Call attention to moments of effectiveness. Highlight why her actions and words are important to teaching and learning. Avoid judgmental or evaluative words ("I liked how you did . . .").

- Invite discussion and reflection. Use open-ended prompts or questions. (For example, "Why did you decide to place the puppets in the dramatic play area?" or "I would like us to talk about nap time, which is a time of day that we have decided to focus on.")

- Guide the teacher to take the next steps. Encourage her to try a new strategy or be more intentional about teaching practices. If appropriate, you might suggest a resource or model a strategy.

- Clarify and confirm. Invite her to summarize the conversation and determine a timetable for the goals you determined together.

- Keep the conversation going. Summarize the conversation in writing. Follow up with an email or phone call.

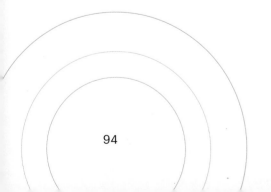

Coaching with Powerful Interactions

Rehearsing a Coaching Conversation

Use this form to prepare for a coaching conversation with a teacher with whom you are establishing a coaching relationship or with whom you have been working.

- Think about the teacher you will be coaching. Record his initials here: _____

- Determine your intention for the meeting. For example, to begin the coaching relationship with the teacher (see example beginning on p. 128) or to identify a goal that the two of you have been focusing on. Jot a note about it here:

_____

_____

_____

_____

1. Make sure you are Present. How might you focus on being calm before the conversation begins?

_____

_____

_____

_____

_____

2. Open to Connect. How might you Connect with the teacher at the beginning of the conversation?

_____

_____

_____

_____

_____

3. Extend Learning

    a. Restate the purpose. What might you say to review the goal you created together?

    b. Present the observation. Read the notes from your observation. Look at photos, video clips, or audio recordings that you captured during your observation.

Validate the teacher's _____. Prepare and rehearse a few "I notice" statements and strengths-based explanations that will make him aware of his moments of effectiveness.

    • I noticed _____.

This is important because _____.

    • I noticed _____.

This is important because _____.

    • I noticed _____.

This is important because _____.

    • I noticed _____.

This is important because _____.

Invite discussion and reflection. Prepare and rehearse a few open-ended prompts or questions. (For example, "I'm curious. How do my observations compare to your own?" Or "During this learning experience, what worked well for you? What worked well for the children? Why do you think so?")

_____

_____

_____

_____

c. Extend the teacher's learning a tiny step forward. Plan and rehearse how you might stretch this teacher forward.

_____

_____

_____

_____

d. Clarify and confirm. What might you say?

_____

_____

_____

e. Keep the conversation going. How might you stay in touch with this teacher?

_____

_____

_____

A Powerful Interactions Introductory Coaching Conversation

In the following dialogue, Jeanne begins to establish a learning partnership with Lynn. She wants to build trust and at the same time set expectations for the relationship. Four ideas Jeanne wants to establish up front are

• Her strengths-based coaching stance

• Having a clear focus for their work together

• The rhythm of their visits—observations and feedback conversations

• Her willingness to individualize to make this work for Lynn

Jeanne: Hi, I'm Jeanne. I'm pleased to meet you. (pause)

Lynn: I'm Lynn.

Jeanne: Hi, Lynn. I'm not sure what you already know about me or my role as a coach. I'd like to tell you what I'm thinking and hear your ideas. (pause)

Lynn: Sounds good.

Jeanne: Our program is fortunate to have a coaching component. My role as coach, as I see it, is to be your learning partner. My approach is to be your mirror—calling attention to the decisions you make that are effective so that you can see them—and then we can talk about them. (pause)

Lynn: (no response)

Jeanne: One coach I know describes her role as shining a flashlight on moments of effectiveness for teachers. You rarely get time to pause and appreciate what you do well. If I call attention to it, highlight it for you, then you can think about more ways you can use your effective strategies with even more intention. (pause)

Lynn: That sounds pretty cool.

Jeanne: Have you worked with a coach before?

Lynn: Not really. My director comes in for evaluation visits.

Jeanne: And then do you get to talk about the visit afterwards?

Lynn: Sometimes. She tells us what we did well and what we need to work on.

Jeanne: Working with a coach is a little different. We will be finding the things you do that are working well for you and the children. We'll think about why those things are working so well, and then think about what you want to do to extend and expand your teaching skills. (pause)

Lynn: Oh. Aren't you here to help me fix the things my director said I need to work on?

Jeanne: I'm here for you. I want to help you appreciate the strengths you already have. Then I want to offer support as you decide on a direction for the next step in your professional growth. What we work on will be up to you.

Lynn: OK. This is not something I've done before, so... [hesitates and then stops]

Jeanne: You may be wondering how coaching works. Here's the plan. We focus on a topic or aspect of your teaching that you choose. I'll visit every two weeks for about 30 minutes of focused observation based on your selected topic. Then I share with you what I've seen, and we discuss the impact of your decisions on children's learning. Having time to process the observation is really important. How does that sound? (pause)

Lynn: It makes sense, but I don't have any time that I can talk with you. My days are really full.

Jeanne: I'm sure that's true. You juggle so many things at one time as an early childhood teacher. (pause)

Lynn: [smiles but says nothing].

Jeanne: We can consider times during the day when we might be able to talk. (pause)

Lynn: Okay. Like what?

Jeanne: Perhaps during nap time for 20 to 30 minutes. Or by email? (pause)

Lynn: I'm not sure.

Jeanne: We can explore options. What's most important is for you to be comfortable with our feedback conversations. If we use nap time, we will sit in the room away from the children so we do not disturb them. Or I can send you an email with my observations—pose a question for you to think about, and you can respond via email. (pause)

Lynn: Okay. Can I think about this?

Jeanne: Of course. It has to work for you. How about we talk by phone in a few days to work out the details of our next interaction? This way you can think about a topic you'd like to focus on first, when would be a good time for me to observe to see you working on the topic, and how we might find a way to have the feedback conversation.

Lynn: Thanks. That sounds okay.

Jeanne: I'd like to call you next Thursday. What's a good time and a number where I can reach you?

Lynn says 3:15 works for her and offers her cell number. The relationship is launched.

Planning for the Feedback Conversation

Use this form to prepare to have a feedback conversation with a teacher after you have observed her in the classroom.

1. Make sure you are Present. Be prepared and calm before the conversation begins. Do a Me Check: Can I quiet the static? How do I need to adjust to find the "just right" fit?

_____

_____

_____

_____

2. Open to Connect. Greet the teacher by name. Thank her for allowing you to visit. Keep a friendly tone to the conversation. Restate the goals and the purpose of the observation and conversation.

_____

_____

_____

_____

3. Extend Learning.

_____

_____

_____

_____

   a. Present the observation. Share a few pieces of strengths-based feedback ("I notice" statements and explanations) that relate to the agreed-upon goals. This will help to validate the teacher, raise her awareness of her moments of effectiveness, and encourage more intentionality in the future.

_____

_____

_____

_____

b. Invite discussion and reflection. Deepen the conversation by using a few open-ended prompts or questions.

_____

_____

_____

_____

c. Guide the teacher to take the next steps. Identify a next step, large or small, to stretch the teacher. You might encourage her to try a new strategy or be more intentional about teaching practices. If appropriate, you might suggest a resource or model a strategy.

_____

_____

_____

_____

d. Clarify and confirm. Double check to be sure about the next step. With the teacher, plan for the next observation.

_____

_____

_____

_____

e. Keep the conversation going. Identify strategies for maintaining contact.

_____

_____

_____

_____

References

Annenberg Institute for School Reform. 2004. Instructional Coaching: Professional Development Strategies That Improve Instruction. Providence, RI: Annenberg Institute for School Reform. http://annenberginstitute.org/pdf/instructionalcoaching.pdf.

Anning, A., & A. Edwards. 2006. *Promoting Children's Learning From Birth to Five: Developing the New Early Years Professional.* 2nd ed. Maidenhead, England: Open University Press.

Barth, R. 2006. "Improving Relationships Within the Schoolhouse." *Educational Leadership* 63 (6): 8–13. www.ascd.org/publications/educational-leadership/mar06/vol63/num06/Improving-Relationships-Within-the-Schoolhouse.aspx.

Broderick, P.C. 2013. "Why Teaching Mindfulness Benefits Students' Learning." MindShift (blog), September 13, 2013. http://blogs.kqed.org/mindshift/2013/09/why-teaching-mindfulness-benefits-students-learning/.

Chao, R. 2009. "Understanding the Adult Learners' Motivation and Barriers to Learning." Paper presented at the ESRA Research Network on Adults Educators, Trainers, and Their Professional Development, Thessaloniki, Greece, November.www.academia.edu/1267765/Understanding_the_Adult_Learners_Motivation_and_Barriers_to_Learning.

Colorado Coaching Consortium. 2009. "Coaching Competencies for Colorado Early Childhood Education." www.cocoaches.net/uploads/Coaching_competencies_Oct_2010.pdf.

Dombro, A.L., J. Jablon, & C. Stetson. 2011. *Powerful Interactions: How to Connect With Children to Extend Their Learning.* Washington, DC: NAEYC.

DuFour, R. 2004. "What Is a 'Professional Learning Community'?" *Educational Leadership* 61 (8): 6–11.

Early, D., O. Barbarin, D. Bryant, M. Burchinal, F. Chang, R. Clifford, G. Crawford, W. Weaver, C. Howes, S. Ritchie, M. Kraft-Sayre, R. Pianta, & W.S. Barnett. 2005. "Pre-Kindergarten in Eleven States: NCEDL's Multi-State Study of Pre-Kindergarten and Study of State-Wide Early Education Programs (SWEEP)." NCEDL Working Paper. Chapel Hill: The University of North Carolina, FPG Child Development Institute, NCEDL. http://fpg.unc.edu/node/4654.

Epstein, A.S. 2014. *The Intentional Teacher: Choosing the Best Strategies for Young Children's Learning.* Rev. ed. Washington, DC: NAEYC; Ypsilanti, MI: HighScope Press.

Gardner, M., & D. Toope. 2011. "A Social Justice Perspective on Strengths-Based Approaches: Exploring Educators' Perspectives and Practices." *Canadian Journal of Education* 34 (3): 89–102.

Hsieh, W., M.L. Hemmeter, J.A. McCollum, & M.M. Ostrosky. 2009. "Using Coaching to Increase Preschool Teachers' Use of Emergent Literacy Teaching Strategies." *Early Childhood Research Quarterly* 24 (3): 229–47.

Kabat-Zinn, J. 2003. "Mindfulness-Based Interventions in Context: Past, Present, and Future." *Clinical Psychology: Science and Practice* 10 (2): 144–56.

Kanter, R.M. 2012. "Ten Reasons People Resist Change." HBR Blog Network (blog), Harvard Business Review, September 25, 2012. http://blogs.hbr.org/2012/09/ten-reasons-people-resist-chang/.

Kissel, B., M. Mraz, B. Algozzine, & K. Stover. 2011. "Early Childhood Literacy Coaches' Role: Perceptions and Recommendations for Change." *Journal of Research in Childhood Education* 25 (3): 288–303.

Langer, E.J. 2009. *Counter Clockwise: Mindful Health and the Power of Possibility.* New York: Ballantine.

Lopez, S.J., & M.C. Louis. 2009. "The Principles of Strengths-Based Education." *Journal of College & Character* 10 (4): 1–8.

Neuman, S., & L. Cunningham. 2009. "The Impact of Professional Development and Coaching on Early Language and Literacy Instructional Practices." *American Educational Research Journal* 46 (2): 532–66.

O'Neill, O. 2013. "How to Trust Intelligently." TED Blog (blog), September 25. http://blog.ted.com/2013/09/25/how-to-trust-intelligently/.

Owen, K.S. 2013. "Hands-On Mentoring of Our First-Year Teachers." *School Administrator* 70 (1): 38–39.

Pawl, J.H., & A.L. Dombro. 2004. *Partnering With Parents to Support Young Children's Development.* Washington, DC: ZERO TO THREE.

Pearson, J., P. Nelson, S. Titsworth, & L. Harter. 2011. *Human Communication.* 4th ed. New York: McGraw-Hill.

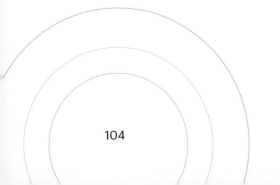

Pianta, R.C. May 25, 2010. "Connecting Early Education to K–3 Through Professional Development for Effective Teaching and Learning." Testimony to the US Senate Health, Education, Labor, and Pensions Committee hearing: ESEA reauthorization: Early childhood education. http://help.senate.gov/imo/media/doc/Pianta.pdf.

Saleebey, D. 1997. *The Strengths Perspective in Social Work Practice.* New York. Longman Publishers.

Saleebey, D. 2013. *The Strengths Perspective in Social Work Practice.* 6th ed. Boston Pearson.

Senge, P.M. 1990. *The Fifth Discipline: The Art and Practice of the Learning Organization.* New York: Doubleday.

Schön, D. 1987. *Educating the Reflective Practitioner: Toward a New Design for Teaching and Learning in the Professions.* San Francisco: Jossey-Bass.

Tompkins, G.E. 2005. *Literacy for the 21st Century.* Upper Saddle River, NJ: Prentice Hall.

Tschannen-Moran, B., & M. Tschannen-Moran. 2011a. "The Coach and the Evaluator." *Educational Leadership* 69 (2): 10–16.

Tschannen-Moran, M., & B. Tschannen-Moran. 2011b. "Taking a Strengths-Based Focus Improves School Climate." *Journal of School Leadership* 21 (3): 422–48.

Vella, S.A., T.P. Crowe, & L.G. Oades. 2013. "Increasing the Effectiveness of Coach Education: Evidence of a Parallel Process." *International Journal of Sports Science and Coaching* 8 (2): 417–30.

Wheatley, M.J. 2001. "Bringing Schools Back to Life: Schools as Living Systems." In *Creating Successful School Systems: Voices From the University, the Field, and the Community*, eds. F.M. Duffy & J.D. Dale. Norwood, MA: Christopher-Gordon Publishers. www.margaretwheatley.com/articles/lifetoschools.html.

About the Authors

Judy, Amy, and Shaun believe that creating ripples of positive change for young children and families requires that we first listen to and learn from teachers, coaches, and program leaders. We then illuminate their moments of effectiveness in professional development conversations, writing, and video.

Judy Jablon supports educators, management teams, schools, and agencies through results-oriented professional development, coaching, consultation, facilitation, and project management. A national authority on early childhood curriculum and assessment, observation techniques, and cross-cultural communication, Judy promotes dialogue and the building of relationships.

Amy Laura Dombro develops resources to assist teachers, family support professionals, and community leaders in their work to create positive change for children and families. Amy translates information so that it is engaging and easy to use and documents stories of successes, challenges, and lessons learned from individuals and programs so that readers can benefit from the experiences of others.

Shaun Johnsen is a television professional with more than 19 years of experience in the field of education. Shaun is a co-owner of Murray Hill Studios, a NYC-based television and webcasting production studio, and uses his unique experiences as a producer, photographer, videographer, editor, and musician to create rich, meaningful content.

At Murray Hill Productions, Judy, Amy, and Shaun collaborate to create videos that invite educators to view their own practice, identify moments of effectiveness, analyze and reinforce these moments, and strategize about how to apply these practices more extensively with greater intention.

Acknowledgments

Creating Coaching with Powerful Interactions has been an exciting collaboration with colleagues with whom we have remarkable relationships and endless Powerful Interactions that continually extend our learning. We express our deep respect and gratitude to each of you who helped us bring this work to fruition.

Charlotte Stetson, coauthor of the first Powerful Interactions book, worked with us to develop many of these ideas. We owe huge thanks to Marc Wein, who had the great idea of introducing Shaun to Judy and early childhood education. We are grateful to Diana Courson, who inspires us with her piercing intellect, thoughtful questions, and wonderful sense of humor. To our friend and collaborator, Laura Ensler, thank you for your wisdom and the many ways you have contributed to our understanding of Powerful Interactions.

Michael Luft engaged with us in the process of learning through videotape and allowed us to capture his voice for others to learn from. We have profound respect for Tychawn Johnson, Helena Pereira, and Sandy Lighter-Jones because of their willingness to be transparent about learning to coach with Powerful Interactions, which helped us to articulate the ideas in this book.

We wish to acknowledge the people and programs who welcomed us and, most important, joined us in conversations about coaching with Powerful Interactions. Our appreciation goes to Diana Courson, Clarissa Wallace, JoAnn Nalley, Eurdora Hardin, Jeanne Duffie, Connie Hicks, Lisa Gaddy, and Megan Bennings of Arkansas State University Childhood Services and affiliated early childhood programs; Tara Evanson, Michael Luft, Lucy Galante, Dana Miuccio, and all the staff of the Ben Samuels Children's Center at Montclair State University in New Jersey; Irene Garneau, Sarah Leibert, Jill Naraine, Shante Lipscomb, Wendy Haller, Amy White, Jenny Levinson, Sue Pike, Jen Treado, and all the teachers at Wintonbury Early Childhood Magnet School in Bloomfield, Connecticut; Sandy Lighter-Jones, Shelli Aiona, Terry Kelly, Deidre Harris, Sally Yuza, and the staff of the early childhood program of the Kamehameha School in Hawaii; Helena Pereira, Karen Cerrabone, Jaquie Onifer, Nancy Ziobro, and the early childhood department staff and preschool teachers of Asbury Park Public Schools in New Jersey; Susan Jacobs, Monica Brinkerhoff, Dana Mulay, Lauren Clark, Angela Zilch, Alan Taylor, Ginger Ward, and all of our colleagues with the Creating Connections Project in Arizona.

Conversations with colleagues are crucial, and they shaped our thinking as we wrote. We wish to acknowledge these individuals for their rich insights and thought-provoking questions: Mark Louis Romei, Jessica Sether, Danielle Yamello, Morgan Casella, Jerlean Daniel, Lisa Rogoff, Jamie Ashton, Heidi Ham, Jacky Howell, Jacquie Gross, Karen Young, Audrey Lassiter, and Grace Radice.

For your assistance with photography, videography, and editing, our gratitude goes to Sandy Lighter-Jones, Helena Pereira, Karen Cerrabone, Michael Griffin, and Bob Harris.

Our colleagues at NAEYC have provided invaluable support to us throughout the process of creating this ebook. Thank you to Kathy Charner, Derry Koralek, Edwin Malstrom, Liz Wegner, Stephanie Morris, and Doug Morrison. We express a special note of thanks to Rhian Evans Allvin for being an advocate for this project.

We want to acknowledge the Powerful Interactions we've shared together throughout the process of creating this book. We took turns quieting our own and each other's static, staying focused on maintaining positive relationships, and connecting with all of the people who helped us bring this work to life. We are grateful for the many ways we've stretched each other's learning over many years of friendship and collaboration.

Finally, the three of us are fortunate to have very special families who inspire us in everything we do. Thank you Andy, Ed, and Jahaneen for your love, support, and guidance. To Darrien, Sasha, and Austin: thank you for reminding us each day how important it is for each of us to remember: "It's all about the children."

—Judy Jablon, Amy Laura Dombro, and Shaun Johnsen

Index

Coaching with Powerful Interactions